Kahoot!
QUIZ TIME
ANIMALS

DK

Contents

Introduction

How many teeth can a crocodile have in its lifetime? What sense is essential for a bird to navigate? How many meerkats live in a colony? Test your animal knowledge in this quiz book, packed with questions and facts.

Featuring everything from desert dwellers and big cats to the adorable pets in your home, celebrate the planet's creatures in all their splendor from the kings of camouflage to record-breaking beasts big and small.

Keep score

Most quizzes in this book have 10 questions each. To keep score, you'll need to record the number of correct answers each player gets after each quiz.

Keep track on a piece of paper or even on a spreadsheet. Be sure to tally up the score for each quiz in order to crown the ultimate winner based on who gets the highest score from all 30 quizzes. Who will grab the gold medal?

Find more quizzes!

Look for QR codes throughout the book. Scan them to find exclusive online quizzes on the same theme. You can also head over to www.kahoot.com to discover more than 100 million quizzes on loads of interesting subjects!

Find 15 QR codes like this one on the pages that follow.

Make your own

Once you've completed these quizzes, get inspired to create your own on kahoot.com!

First, plan out your questions on paper and check out our top tips to make your quiz the best it can be. When it's ready, share your quiz with friends and family.

Don't worry about who wins or if your quiz doesn't turn out exactly how you planned. The important thing is to have fun . . . but it's even more important to stay safe online. Never share any personal information with anyone online and always use the internet with a trusted adult.

Top tips

1 Do your research and always check your facts with three trusted online sources.

2 Give your quiz a fun theme and vary your questions so the quiz doesn't get repetitive.

3 Include three or four multiple choice options, plus a few true or false and picture rounds.

Pets

Can you and your pet whizz through this quiz? With a stroke of luck, you'll know lots of the answers!

1 What are the most common pets?
- ◆ Cats and dogs
- ▲ Rabbits and hamsters
- ● Guinea pigs and goldfish

2 Which of these things do pets not need from their owners?
- ◆ Water
- ▲ Food
- ● Shelter
- ■ Disco dancing

3 True or false: Domestic dogs are descended from wolves.
- ◆ True
- ▲ False

5 What's the preferred diet for a pet corn snake?
- ◆ Live mice
- ▲ Dead mice
- ● Grass

4 Rabbits eat their own poo! What else is rabbit poo known as?
- ◆ Cecotrophs
- ▲ Bunny currants
- ● Lawn chocolates

Did you know?

Egyptians used the Nile goose as a guard pet to protect their homes and livestock.

6 Goldfish were first bred in China, but how many years ago?
- ◆ Over 4,500 years ago
- ▲ Over 12,000 years ago
- ● Over 50,000 years ago

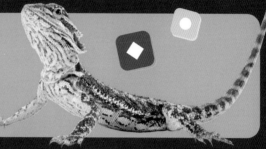

7 How big can a giant African land snail grow to?
- ◆ 7.9 in (20 cm)
- ▲ 11.8 in (30 cm)
- ● 15.7 in (40 cm)

8 Which of these is not a species of hamster?
- ◆ Russian Dwarf
- ▲ Roborovski
- ● Robot Ham

9 How long can a bearded dragon live to in captivity?
- ◆ 5–10 years
- ▲ 10–15 years
- ● 20–25 years

10 Can you tell what this pet is from the picture?
- ◆ Lizard
- ▲ Tortoise
- ● Hedgehog

Scan the QR code for a Kahoot! about pets.

Turn to page 8 for the answers!

Pets

Answers

1 What are the most common pets?

◆ Cats and dogs

On average, 33 percent of households in the world have a dog while 23 percent have a cat.

2 Which of these things do pets not need from their owners?

■ Disco dancing

Some pets do need exercise, but walking is a better way to do this!

3 True or false: Domestic dogs are descended from wolves.

◆ True

The domestic dog diverged from a species of wolf more than 10,000 years ago.

4 Rabbits eat their own poo! What else is rabbit poo known as?

◆ Cecotrophs

They pass the poo and then eat it to make sure all the nutrients are absorbed.

5 What's the preferred diet for a pet corn snake?

▲ Dead mice

In the wild they hunt a variety of live prey, but as pets, dead mice are their favorite food.

6 Goldfish were first bred in China, but how many years ago?

◆ Over 4,500 years ago

Goldfish were brought to England in the 18th century and have remained the most popular coldwater pet fish.

7 How big can a giant African land snail grow to?

◆ 7.9 in (20 cm)

That's about the same size as a banana! These snails will eat at least 500 different types of plants.

8 Which of these is not a species of hamster?

● Robot Ham

There are 24 species of hamster in total.

9 How long can a bearded dragon live to in captivity?

▲ 10–15 years

The name bearded dragon comes from the spiky folds of skin around the reptile's neck, which inflate and turn black when they feel excited or threatened.

10 Can you tell what this pet is from the picture?

▲ Tortoise

Podium!
Bronze: 1–5 correct answers
Silver: 6–8 correct answers
Gold: 9–10 correct answers

Jungle

Go deep into the jungle and test out what you know. This quiz will have you swinging from the trees!

1 How long can giant centipedes grow up to?
- ◆ 5.9 in (15 cm)
- ▲ 11.8 in (30 cm)
- ● 19.7 in (50 cm)
- ■ 26 in (66 cm)

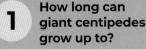

2 Monkeys have two arms and legs, but what do some species use as a "fifth limb" to help them climb trees?
- ◆ Their ears
- ▲ Their tail
- ● Their fur

3 True or false: The task of cataloging invertebrates in the jungle will never be complete.
- ◆ True
- ▲ False

4 Put these jungle animals in order of loudness!
- ◆ Howler monkey
- ▲ Tree frog
- ● Cicada
- ■ Kakapo parrot

Did you know?
The animal species in the jungle outnumber those of all other land habitats combined.

5 Which of these animals are vegetarian?
- ◆ Sloths
- ▲ Anteaters
- ● Armadillos

7 Which of these is not from the parrot family?
- ◆ Parakeet
- ▲ Macaw
- ● Cockatoo
- ■ Toucan

6 How do fruit bats help rainforests grow?
- ◆ They spread seeds from the fruit they eat
- ▲ They dig holes and plant
- ● They fly over and check where plants need to go

8 What gives the eyelash pit viper its name?
- ◆ Raised scales above the eyes that look like eyelashes
- ▲ Actual eyelashes
- ● Claws above the eyes that look like eyelashes

9 Atlas moths have huge wings. How big can their wingspan get?
- ◆ 6.7 in (17 cm)
- ▲ 7.9 in (20 cm)
- ● 10.6 in (27 cm)

10 What animal is this?
- ◆ Red-eyed tree frog
- ▲ Emerald tree boa
- ● Chameleon

Turn to page 12 for the answers!

Jungle Answers

1 How long can giant centipedes grow up to?

▲ 11.8 in (30 cm)

They can overpower and eat tarantulas!

2 Monkeys have two arms and legs, but what do some species use as a "fifth limb" to help them climb trees?

▲ Their tail

Most monkeys have tails longer than their bodies.

3 True or false: The task of cataloging invertebrates in the jungle will never be complete.

◆ True

Most large tropical animals have been identified, but there are just too many!

4 Put these jungle animals in order of loudness!

◆ Howler monkey
● Cicada
■ Kakapo parrot
▲ Tree frog

The booming calls of the South American howler monkeys are the loudest noises made by any land animal on Earth.

5 Which of these animals are vegetarian?

◆ Sloths

They mainly eat leaves of a limited number of tree species. Anteaters are insectivorous. Armadillos are omnivores!

6 **How do fruit bats help rainforests grow?**

◆ They spread seeds from the fruit they eat

The fruit bats carry seeds in them as they digest their food and excrete them far away.

7 **Which of these is not from the parrot family?**

■ Toucan

Parrots have a large head with a strongly hooked bill. Toucans have a smaller head with a very large, distinctive bill.

8 **What gives the eyelash pit viper its name?**

◆ Raised scales above the eyes that look like eyelashes

It's a nocturnal hunter, using the heat pits between its eyes and nostrils to help it to locate prey in the dark.

9 **Atlas moths have huge wings. How big can their wingspan get?**

● 10.6 in (27 cm)

Once they're fully grown the adult moths don't eat!

10 **What animal is this?**

◆ Red-eyed tree frog

By day, a red-eyed tree frog hides by clinging to the underside of a leaf. Concealing its bright orange feet and blue legs beneath its green body it closes its red eyes, and stays perfectly still.

Podium!

Bronze: 1–5 correct answers

Silver: 6–8 correct answers

Gold: 9–10 correct answers

Big Cats

Complete this purr-fect quiz and find out if you're equal to an ace predator.

1 What is a group of tigers called?
- ◆ A troop
- ▲ An ambush
- ● A pride

2 Which big cat is a species of leopard but called something quite different?
- ◆ Tiger
- ▲ Cheetah
- ● Black panther

3 Which big cat is most endangered?
- ◆ The snow leopard
- ▲ The Amur tiger
- ● The African lion

4 How fast can a cheetah run?
- ◆ 58 mph (93 kph)
- ▲ 52 mph (83 kph)
- ● 64 mph (103 kph)

5 Who can eat more in a single meal?
- ◆ Lion
- ▲ Tiger

Did you know?

A tiger's night vision is at least six times better than a human's.

6 How far away can an adult male lion's roar be heard?
- ◆ 3.7 miles (6 km)
- ▲ 4.3 miles (7 km)
- ● 5 miles (8 km)

7 True or false: A tiger has retractable claws that spring out when it seizes prey.
- ◆ True
- ▲ False

8 Who are the main hunters in a pride of lions?
- ◆ The lions
- ▲ The lionesses

9 About how long will a cheetah chase its prey for?
- ◆ 45 seconds
- ▲ 4.5 minutes
- ● 45 minutes

10 Where are jaguars from?
- ◆ Central America and South America
- ▲ East and Southeast Asia
- ● Africa and South Asia

Scan the QR code for a Kahoot! about big cats.

Turn to page 16 for the answers!

Big Cats Answers

1 **What is a group of tigers called?**
▲ An ambush
They can also be known as a streak of tigers.

2 **Which big cat is a species of leopard but called something quite different?**
● Black panther
Its real name is a melanic leopard. The skin and fur of leopards contain large amounts of the dark pigment, melanin. In deserts, leopards are pale yellow; in grass, they are deeper yellow. In forests they are black (melanic panthers).

3 **Which big cat is most endangered?**
▲ The Amur tiger
There are thought to be only around 500 left in the wild. There are around 6,500 snow leopards and 20,000 African lions.

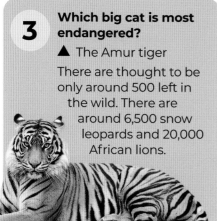

4 **How fast can a cheetah run?**
◆ 58 mph (93 kph)
No animal can run faster than a cheetah. This highly specialized cat is uniquely adapted for accelerating faster than most sports cars.

5. Who can eat more in a single meal?

▲ Tiger

It can eat 110 lb of meat (50 kg). A lion can eat 88 lb (40 kg), but then can go three or four days without eating.

6. How far away can an adult male lion's roar be heard?

● 5 miles (8 km)

Lions roar to warn others away from their territory, and to show how powerful they are.

7. True or false: A tiger has retractable claws that spring out when it seizes prey.

◆ True

Normally its claws are retracted when moving around to keep them sharp.

8. Who are the main hunters in a pride of lions?

▲ The lionesses

They stalk prey before launching an attack, and often work together to surround an animal and cut off its escape.

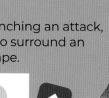

9. About how long will a cheetah chase its prey for?

◆ 45 seconds

It can lose its prey to other big cats as it can't keep going for as long.

10. Where are jaguars from?

◆ Central America and South America

Jaguars are the largest of the big cats in South America and the third largest in the world.

Podium!

Bronze: 1–5 correct answers
Silver: 6–8 correct answers
Gold: 9–10 correct answers

Desert

Don't desert this quiz! Give it a go to find out about the creatures that dwell in the driest places on Earth.

1 How do marsupial and golden moles get around in the desert?
- ◆ They fly over the sand
- ▲ They have extra-large feet to help them move over sand
- ● They move through the sand and not on top

2 Which fox lives in the Sahara and Sahel regions of Africa?
- ◆ Fennec fox
- ▲ Arctic fox
- ● Red fox

3 How many insects can the thorny devil lizard consume in one meal?
- ◆ 250
- ▲ 2,500
- ● 25,000
- ■ 45,000

Did you know?
Antarctica and the Arctic are actually polar deserts. That makes the polar bear a desert animal!

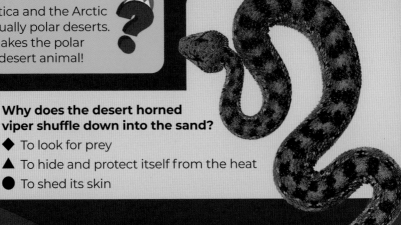

4 Why does the desert horned viper shuffle down into the sand?
- ◆ To look for prey
- ▲ To hide and protect itself from the heat
- ● To shed its skin

5 What bird species is the roadrunner related to?
- ◆ The ostrich
- ▲ The emu
- ● The cuckoo

6 How many meerkats live in a colony?
- ◆ 3–20
- ▲ 10–30
- ● 50–100

7 How much can a swarm of 50 billion locusts eat in one day?
- ◆ 1,123 tons (1,000 tonnes)
- ▲ 11,231 tons (10,000 tonnes)
- ● 110,231 tons (100,000 tonnes)

8 How do desert kangaroos and wallabies cool themselves down?
- ◆ They spit at each other
- ▲ They lick themselves
- ● They endlessly search for water

9 Why are most desert animals active after dark?
- ◆ Because temperatures in the day can reach up to 158°F (70°C)
- ▲ Because they can't see in the daytime
- ● Because they like to look at the moon while eating

Turn to page 20 for the answers!

Desert Answers

1 How do marsupial and golden moles get around in the desert?

● They move through the sand and not on top

Other desert animals like camels and geckos have extra-large feet that help them move over sand.

2 Which fox lives in the Sahara and Sahel regions of Africa?

◆ Fennec fox

It's the smallest member of the dog family and its furred soles are adapted for walking on hot, soft sand.

3 How many insects can the thorny devil lizard consume in one meal?

▲ 2,500

It eats during the day when ants are on the move.

4 Why does the desert horned viper shuffle down into the sand?

▲ To hide and protect itself from the heat

When it spots prey the viper will pursue it into its burrow.

6 How many meerkats live in a colony?

◆ 3–20

They enlarge the former burrows of ground squirrels.

5 What bird species is the roadrunner related to?

● The cuckoo

It can reach speeds of 18 mph (30 kph) running through the desert.

8 How do desert kangaroos and wallabies cool themselves down?

▲ They lick themselves

The saliva cools them down as it evaporates. Other desert animals such as lizards and snakes are often described as "cold-blooded." This actually means that their body temperature rises and falls with that of their surroundings.

7 How much can a swarm of 50 billion locusts eat in one day?

● 110,231 tons (100,000 tonnes)

Each locust can eat its weight in plants in a single day.

9 Why are most desert animals active after dark?

◆ Because temperatures in the day can reach up to 158°F (70°C)

As a result most animals hide away, leaving little sign of themselves apart from tracks.

Podium!

Bronze: 1–4 correct answers

Silver: 5–7 correct answers

Gold: 8–9 correct answers

Reptiles

Do you know your snakes from your lizards? Can you take on a crocodile and win? Time to get quizzing!

1 Which reptile is renowned for its ability to change color?
- ◆ Chameleon
- ▲ Sea snake
- ● Alligator

2 How many species of lizard and snakes are there?
- ◆ 9,905
- ▲ 10,855
- ● 8,765

3 What is a tuatara?
- ◆ It is the only survivor of a group of reptiles that were alive at the same time as dinosaurs
- ▲ It is a type of tree
- ● It is a type of dance

4 Put these crocodilians in order of length.
- ◆ American alligator
- ▲ Nile crocodile
- ● Saltwater crocodile
- ■ Dwarf crocodile

5 What is the oldest age a Galápagos tortoise is thought to have lived?
- ◆ 120 years old
- ▲ 150 years old
- ● 170 years old

Did you know?
The biggest group of land animals that has ever lived were reptiles—the dinosaurs.

6 Which of these turtles is a herbivore?
- ◆ Stinkpot turtle
- ▲ Green sea turtle
- ● Leatherback sea turtle

7 How do most reptiles reproduce?
- ◆ They give birth to live young
- ▲ They lay eggs

8 How big can a Komodo dragon grow?
- ◆ Up to 7.5 ft (2.3 m)
- ▲ Up to 10.2 ft (3.1 m)
- ● Up to 17 ft (5.2 m)

9 How fast can the emerald tree boa move?
- ◆ Fast enough to snatch birds out of the air
- ▲ Fast enough to catch birds sitting on branches
- ● Fast enough to catch birds just as they take off

Scan the QR code for a Kahoot! about reptiles.

10 True or false: All living reptiles are cold-blooded vertebrates with tough, waterproof skins.
- ◆ True
- ▲ False

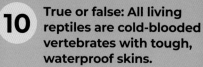

Turn to page 24 for the answers!

Reptiles
Answers

1 Which reptile is renowned for its ability to change color?
- ◆ Chameleon

They also possess long, sticky-tipped tongues, which can shoot out to enormous lengths.

2 How many species of lizard and snakes are there?
- ◆ 9,905

They are the largest order of reptiles.

3 What is a tuatara?
- ◆ It is the only survivor of a group of reptiles that were alive at the same time as dinosaurs

This group mostly died out 100 million years ago. It lives in New Zealand.

4 Put these crocodilians in order of length.
- ■ Dwarf crocodile is up to 6.5 ft (2 m)
- ◆ American alligator is up to 16.4 ft (5 m)
- ▲ Nile crocodile is up to 20 ft (6.1 m)
- ● Saltwater crocodile is up to 23 ft (7 m)

5 What is the oldest age a Galápagos tortoise is thought to have lived?

● 170 years old

They are the largest tortoises on Earth.

6 Which of these turtles is a herbivore?

▲ Green sea turtle

The others eat seafood. Turtles and tortoises date back to more than 220 million years ago!

7 How do most reptiles reproduce?

▲ They lay eggs

Only a few, like boa snakes and vipers, give birth to live young.

8 How big can a Komodo dragon grow?

▲ Up to 10.2 ft (3.1 m)

Its venomous bite makes escape very difficult for its victims.

9 How fast can the emerald tree boa move?

◆ Fast enough to snatch birds out of the air

It seizes prey in its extra-long teeth, then squeezes it to death.

Podium!

Bronze: 1–5 correct answers
Silver: 6–8 correct answers
Gold: 9–10 correct answers

10 True or false: All living reptiles are cold-blooded vertebrates with tough, waterproof skins.

◆ True

It allows them to survive in some of the driest places on Earth.

Mountain

Journey high into the mountains and test your ability to quiz at altitude. Hold on!

1 Which sheep live on rugged mountainous terrain?
- ◆ Bighead sheep
- ▲ Bighorn sheep
- ● Bigfoot sheep

2 How high up have yaks been found in the Himalayas?
- ◆ 13,120 ft (4,000 m)
- ▲ 19,800 ft (6,000 m)
- ● 26,246 ft (8,000 m)

3 How do the snow leopard's feet equip it to live at high altitudes?
- ◆ They are very furry
- ▲ They are very hard
- ● They are very big

4 How long can the Andean condor soar for without beating its wings?
- ◆ Ten minutes
- ▲ Half an hour
- ● An hour

Did you know?
Mountain chickens are not chickens and they don't live in the mountains. They are one of the world's largest species of frog, sometimes growing to over 8 in (20 cm) and weighing up to 2 lb (1 kg).

5 How long do Alpine marmots spend in hibernation?
◆ Half the year
▲ A quarter of the year
● A third of the year

6 How high do mountain hummingbirds in South America feed?
◆ Over 6,561 ft (2,000 m)
▲ Over 9,842 ft (3,000 m)
● Over 13,200 ft (4,000 m)

7 The high-living relative of the camel, the vicuña, has how many more red blood cells than other mammals?
◆ 3 times
▲ 6 times
● 10 times

8 True or false: Birds cope with high altitudes because air passes through their lungs in only one direction.
◆ True
▲ False

9 How is the eastern mountain gorilla different than its lowland cousins?
◆ It has longer arms
▲ It has long, shaggy fur
● It has a bigger head

10 Why do red deer spend the summer in the mountains and migrate down in the autumn?
◆ The autumn is the mating season
▲ They don't like getting cold
● They want to go on holiday

Turn to page 28 for the answers!

Mountain Answers

1 Which sheep live on rugged mountainous terrain?

▲ Bighorn sheep

The rams are famous for their large curled horns.

2 How high up have yaks been found in the Himalayas?

▲ 19,800 ft (6,000 m)

One of the few animals that have adapted to life at such an altitude, yaks graze grasses, herbs, mosses, and lichens, and use ice or snow as a source of water.

3 How do the snow leopard's feet equip it to live at high altitudes?

◆ They are very furry

They help to prevent the cat losing heat through its feet, and may improve its grip on bare rock.

4 How long can the Andean condor soar for without beating its wings?

● An hour

It outspreads its huge wings to ride updrafts on.

5 How long do Alpine marmots spend in hibernation?

◆ Half the year

This is one of the longest periods of dormancy for any mammal.

6 How high do mountain hummingbirds in South America feed?

◆ Over 6,561 ft (2,000 m)

It gets very cold at night, so the birds slow their heart rates and drop their body temperature rather than try to keep warm.

7 The high-living relative of the camel, the vicuña, has how many more red blood cells than other mammals?

◆ 3 times

The hemoglobin in their red blood cells is unusually good at collecting oxygen.

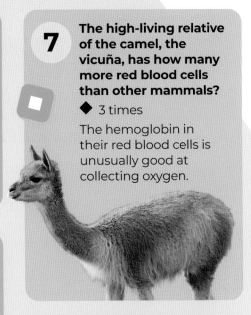

8 True or false: Birds cope with high altitudes because air passes through their lungs in only one direction.

◆ True

Air has half the normal amount of oxygen at 19,800 ft (6,000 m) above sea level. Far more oxygen enters a bird's bloodstream than a mammal's at this altitude.

9 How is the eastern mountain gorilla different than its lowland cousins?

◆ It has longer arms

It uses the dense vegetation of the forest zone for both food and cover.

10 Why do red deer spend the summer in the mountains and migrate down in the autumn?

◆ The autumn is the mating season

During the summer, food is plentiful up in the mountains and there are relatively few biting flies.

Podium!

Bronze: 1–5 correct answers
Silver: 6–8 correct answers
Gold: 9–10 correct answers

Rock Pools

Find out if your knowledge is solid as a rock with this quiz. Come on, grab a bucket and roll up your pants!

1 Which animal does not live in a rock pool?
- ◆ Urchin
- ▲ Toucan
- ● Periwinkle
- ■ Sea star

2 What type of crab lives inside discarded sea snail shells?
- ◆ Hermit crab
- ▲ Fiddler crab
- ● Spider crab

3 True or false: The water in rock pools is saltier than the sea.
- ◆ True
- ▲ False

5 Which of these rock pool creatures does not have a shell?
- ◆ Anemone
- ▲ Winkle
- ● Sea urchin
- ■ Painted topshell

4 Which of these is an aquatic snail with a cone shaped shell?
- ◆ Limpet
- ▲ Crumpet
- ● Octopus

Did you know?
Rock pools can be as deep as 8 ft (2.5 m). That's taller than an adult male human.

6 Why do small fish called blennies have eyes near the top of their heads?
- ◆ To look appealing to other fish
- ▲ To check what the weather is doing
- ● To look out for attacking sea birds

7 How many different species of sea star are there?
- ◆ Less than 10
- ▲ Up to 100
- ● More than 1,000

8 True or false: Sea stars can never have more than five arms.
- ◆ True
- ▲ False

9 Why do anemones wave their tentacles around in the water?
- ◆ To find a mate
- ▲ To catch prey
- ● To keep predators away

10 What is seaweed?
- ◆ Plant
- ▲ Algae
- ● Animal

Scan the QR code for a Kahoot! about rock pools.

Turn to page 32 for the answers!

Rock Pools
Answers

1 Which animal does not live in a rock pool?

▲ Toucan

These colorful birds live in tropical forests.

2 What type of crab lives inside discarded sea snail shells?

◆ Hermit crab

As they can't grow their own shells for protection, hermit crabs inhabit the discarded shells of other sea creatures.

3 True or false: The water in rock pools is saltier than the sea.

◆ True

Rock pools are harsh environments. The sun's heat makes the water warmer and saltier than the sea.

4 Which of these is an aquatic snail with a cone shaped shell?

◆ Limpet

Limpets have rows of microscopic teeth that they use to scrape vegetation from rocks.

5 Which of these rock pool creatures does not have a shell?

◆ Anemone

These shell-less colorful creatures have venom-filled tentacles.

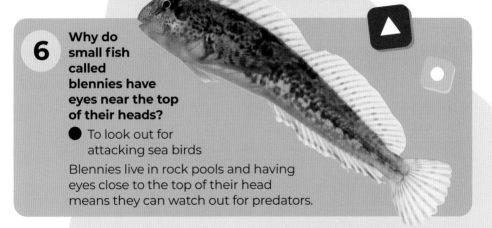

6 Why do small fish called blennies have eyes near the top of their heads?

● To look out for attacking sea birds

Blennies live in rock pools and having eyes close to the top of their head means they can watch out for predators.

7 How many different species of sea star are there?

● More than 1,000

There are about 1,600 species of sea star in the oceans around the world.

8 True or false: Sea stars can never have more than five arms.

▲ False

Most sea stars have five arms, but some species can have up to 50 arms.

9 Why do anemones wave their tentacles around in the water?

▲ To catch prey

Anemones catch floating food this way.

10 What is seaweed?

▲ Algae

Although seaweed looks like a plant, it is algae. It has no roots, stem, or leaves.

Podium!

Bronze: 1–5 correct answers
Silver: 6–8 correct answers
Gold: 9–10 correct answers

Transformers

They say that a change is as good as a rest, now go put that to the test . . .

1 Where do caterpillars change into butterflies?

◆ Inside a chrysanthemum

▲ Inside a chrysalis

● On a crystal ball

2 What animal can make itself younger?

◆ Bumblebee

▲ Immortal jellyfish

● Chameleon

3 True or false: Chameleons change color to blend in with their surroundings.

◆ True

▲ False

4 Why do some sea anemones tuck their tentacles up inside their bodies during low tide?

◆ To look pretty

▲ To confuse predators

● To stay moist

■ For camouflage

Did you know?
The tadpole stage (before turning into a frog) can be as short as two weeks.

5 What is the biological name for when an animal transforms as part of its life cycle?
- ◆ Disguise
- ▲ Metamorphosis
- ● Metabolism
- ■ Fancy dress

6 Put these in order to show the life cycle of a butterfly transforming.
- ◆ Pupa
- ▲ Larva
- ● Adult
- ■ Egg

7 Which of these is famous for its ability to disguise itself?
- ◆ Chameleon octopus
- ▲ Mimic octopus
- ● Theatrical octopus

9 Which animal can change its skin texture as disguise?
- ◆ Frog
- ▲ Cuttlefish
- ● Tiger
- ■ Lemur

8 What is the reason an animal transforms as part of its life cycle?
- ◆ To stop them getting bored
- ▲ To confuse other animals
- ● To help them find food

Turn to page 36 for the answers!

Transformers
Answers

1 **Where do caterpillars change into butterflies?**
▲ Inside a chrysalis
This is a hardened case that protects the creature during the transformation process.

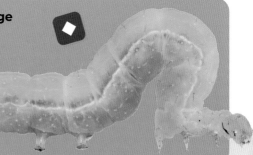

2 **What animal can make itself younger?**
▲ Immortal jellyfish
Like all jellyfish, it begins life as an egg, then a polyp, then a jellyfish. But it can revert back to a polyp whenever it likes and start again.

3 **True or false: Chameleons change color to blend in with their surroundings.**
▲ False
Color changes happen because of temperature, light, and as a way to express emotions.

4 **Why do some sea anemones tuck their tentacles up inside their bodies during low tide?**
● To stay moist
Some sea anemones retract their tentacles to prevent them from drying out before the tide comes back in.

5 What is the biological name for when an animal transforms as part of its life cycle?

▲ Metamorphosis

This is the name for when animals totally change their form when they mature into adulthood. It allows them to live in different ways and in different habitats.

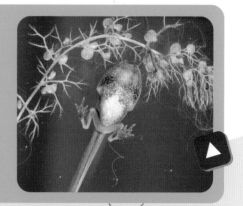

6 Put these in order to show the life cycle of a butterfly transforming.

■ Egg
▲ Larva (caterpillar)
◆ Pupa (chrysalis)
● Adult (butterfly)

7 Which of these is famous for its ability to disguise itself?

▲ Mimic octopus

This octopus can disguise itself as a number of different creatures, including sea snakes and lionfish.

8 What is the reason an animal transforms as part of its life cycle?

● To help them find food

These changes allow animals to live in different habitats, travel, and hunt more easily for food.

Podium!

Bronze: 1–4 correct answers
Silver: 5–7 correct answers
Gold: 8–9 correct answers

9 Which animal can change its skin texture as disguise?

▲ Cuttlefish

Cuttlefish use special muscles to blend in with their surroundings.

Sea

Are you ready for a deep dive into this quiz all about saltwater creatures?

1 Which is the largest of all the seals?
◆ Elephant seal
▲ Leopard seal
● Ringed seal

2 What are corals in reefs made from?
◆ Rocks
▲ Shells
● Animals
■ Plants

3 True or false: Jellyfish have no heart, brain, bones, or eyes.
◆ True
▲ False

4 What do bottlenose dolphins do to look out for predators?
◆ Take turns to sleep
▲ Sleep with one eye open
● Build a nest
■ Only sleep in the daytime

5 How do anglerfish catch their prey?
- ◆ They hide in the sand
- ▲ They blow bubbles
- ● They use a lure like a fishing line

6 Why do octopuses fire inky liquid from their body?
- ◆ As self-defense
- ▲ As a celebration
- ● To show they're tired

7 How big is a wandering albatross' wingspan?
- ◆ 5 ft (1.5 m)
- ▲ 11.4 ft (3.5 m)
- ● 18 ft (5.5 m)

Did you know?
Jellyfish have been around since before the days of the dinosaurs— that's millions of years!

8 Which creature doesn't eat for most of the year?
- ◆ Humpback whale
- ▲ Sea star
- ● Jellyfish
- ■ Basking shark

Scan the QR code for a Kahoot! about sea creatures.

Turn to page 40 for the answers!

9 How many hearts does an octopus have?
- ◆ One
- ▲ Two
- ● Three
- ■ Four

Sea

Answers

1 Which is the largest of all the seals?
◆ Elephant seal
Males can be over 20 ft (6 m) long and they can weigh up to 8,800 lb (3,990 kg).

2 What are corals in reefs made from?
● Animals
They are called polyps and they live and grow while connected to one another in a colony.

3 True or false: Jellyfish have no heart, brain, bones, or eyes.
◆ True
They have a sack-like body and tentacles that are packed with stinging cells.

4 What do bottlenose dolphins do to look out for predators?
▲ Sleep with one eye open
Only one half of a bottlenose dolphin's brain sleeps at a time. They always keep one eye open. This means they can look out for predators.

5 How do anglerfish catch their prey?

● They use a lure like a fishing line

The females suspend a lure near their mouths to attract small prey.

6 Why do octopuses fire inky liquid from their body?

◆ As self-defense

The inky fluid darkens the water, making it hard for predators to see the octopus as it swims to safety.

7 How big is a wandering albatross' wingspan?

▲ 11.4 ft (3.5 m)

These sea birds rely on their huge wings to glide for thousands of miles.

8 Which creature doesn't eat for most of the year?

◆ Humpback whale

Humpbacks living in the southern hemisphere live on their fat reserves for up to seven and a half months of the year.

9 How many hearts does an octopus have?

● Three

Two hearts pump blood through the gills to pick up oxygen, and the third circulates the oxygenated blood through the body.

Podium!

Bronze: 1–4 correct answers

Silver: 5–7 correct answers

Gold: 8–9 correct answers

Sharks

No doubt you'll chomp your way through this shark quiz. That's the tooth!

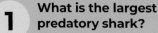

1 What is the largest predatory shark?
- ◆ Tiger shark
- ▲ Whale shark
- ● Great white shark
- ■ Spiny dogfish

2 What is the name of the fin on a shark's back that can poke out of the water?
- ◆ Pectoral fin
- ▲ Dorsal fin
- ● Pelvic fin

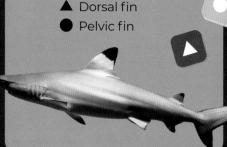

3 What is the length of a shark's pregnancy?
- ◆ 9 months
- ▲ Up to a year
- ● Up to two years

4 What is a group of sharks called?
- ◆ Flock
- ▲ School
- ● Gaggle

Did you know?
Sharks are always growing new teeth. Some species have a new set every two weeks.

5 True or false: A shark's skeleton is made of cartilage.
- ◆ True
- ▲ False

6 What are baby sharks called?
- ◆ Calves
- ▲ Cubs
- ● Kits
- ■ Pups

7 How do sharks breathe?
- ◆ Using grills
- ▲ Through their gills
- ● With their frills

8 How did cookiecutter sharks get their name?
- ◆ They smell sweet
- ▲ From the shape of the wounds they make
- ● From their size

9 How many rows of teeth does a bull shark have?
- ◆ 5
- ▲ 15
- ● 25
- ■ 50

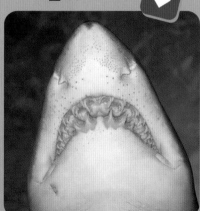

10 Why is a mako shark blue?
- ◆ Because it mainly eats blue fish
- ▲ To keep it hidden against the color of the ocean
- ● Because it's always sad

Turn to page 44 for the answers!

Sharks Answers

1 What is the largest predatory shark?

● Great white shark

It can weigh more than 2.4 tons (2.2 tonnes) and can eat seals whole.

2 What is the name of the fin on a shark's back that can poke out of the water?

▲ Dorsal fin

This pointed fin keeps the shark upright and stops it from rolling over.

3 What is the length of a shark's pregnancy?

● Up to two years

Unlike humans, who are pregnant for nine months, female sharks are pregnant for two years.

4 What is a group of sharks called?

▲ School

Hammerhead sharks live in a group or "school" of up to 100 sharks.

5 **True or false: A shark's skeleton is made of cartilage.**

◆ True

Cartilage is less dense than bone, and this means sharks can move quickly through water with less effort.

6 **What are baby sharks called?**

■ Pups

Just like seal and dolphin babies, shark babies are called pups.

7 **How do sharks breathe?**

▲ Through their gills

Sharks take in oxygen from the water through their gills.

8 **How did cookiecutter sharks get their name?**

▲ From the shape of the wounds they make

They use their sharp, pointy teeth to bite chunks of cookie-shaped flesh from prey.

9 **How many rows of teeth does a bull shark have?**

■ 50

Average sharks have up to 15 rows of teeth, so this makes bull sharks among the most dangerous.

10 **Why is a mako shark blue?**

▲ To keep it hidden against the color of the ocean

The blue color acts as camouflage and helps it to creep up on prey without warning.

Podium!

Bronze: 1–5 correct answers
Silver: 6–8 correct answers
Gold: 9–10 correct answers

Rainforest

Here's hoping you can see the wood for the trees in this fun rainforest quiz.

1 Why are spider monkeys called spider monkeys?
- ◆ They're closely related to spiders
- ▲ They look like spiders
- ● They have eight legs
- ■ They spin webs

2 Which of these rainforest creatures is a primate?
- ◆ Woolly monkey
- ▲ Lemur
- ● Scarlet macaw

3 What does the color of poison dart frogs tell us?
- ◆ Their mood
- ▲ Whether they're hungry
- ● How toxic they are

4 Put these rainforest animals in order from smallest to biggest.
- ◆ Orangutan
- ▲ Sloth
- ● Vampire bat
- ■ Giant anteater

Did you know?

Anteaters are excellent swimmers and they use their long noses as snorkels.

5 What percentage of genes do humans share with chimpanzees?
◆ 68 percent
▲ 78 percent
● 88 percent
■ 98 percent

6 What surprising thing does the binturong smell of?
◆ Leaves
▲ Buttered popcorn
● Roast dinner

7 True or false: The orangutan has a tail.
◆ True
▲ False

8 How many hours does a sloth sleep for every day?
◆ Up to 10 hours
▲ Up to 15 hours
● Up to 20 hours
■ More than 20 hours

9 Which of the below is a type of rainforest wild cat?
◆ Siamang
▲ South American coati
● Ocelot
■ Okapi

10 Which of the below is a huge rodent native to South America?
◆ Capybara
▲ Sloth
● Lemur

Scan the QR code for a Kahoot! about rainforest animals.

Turn to page 48 for the answers!

Rainforest
Answers

1 Why are spider monkeys called spider monkeys?

▲ They look like spiders
These monkeys look a bit like spiders when they hang from trees by their tail with their long arms and legs.

2 Which of these rainforest creatures is a primate?

◆ Woolly monkey
With their short and thick fur, these primates of the western Amazon river basin are very distinctive.

3 What does the color of poison dart frogs tell us?

● How toxic they are
The color of poison dart frogs is a warning to potential predators that they are toxic and won't taste good.

4 Put these rainforest animals in order from smallest to biggest.

● Vampire bat 3.5 in (9 cm)
▲ Sloth 23 in (58 cm)
■ Giant anteater 47 in (120 cm)
◆ Orangutan 53 in (136 cm)

5 What percentage of genes do humans share with chimpanzees?

■ 98 percent
Chimpanzees are our closest cousins. Like humans, chimps are social and care for their offspring for many years.

6
What surprising thing does the binturong smell of?

▲ Buttered popcorn

Binturongs look like a cross between a bear and a cat. They mark their territory with a popcorn scented aroma.

7
True or false: The orangutan has a tail.

▲ False

Orangutans are apes. They swing through trees with ease thanks to their long fingers and toes.

8
How many hours does a sloth sleep for every day?

● Up to 20 hours

Sloths are either asleep or moving very slowly— so slowly that algae grows on their fur.

9
Which of the below is a type of rainforest wild cat?

● Ocelot

This nocturnal wild cat's spotted coat helps it blend in with the rainforest habitat so it can sleep safely during the day.

10
Which of the below is a huge rodent native to South America?

◆ Capybara

These rainforest dwellers look a bit like big guinea pigs and are the world's largest rodent.

Podium!
Bronze: 1–5 correct answers
Silver: 6–8 correct answers
Gold: 9–10 correct answers

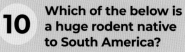

Migration

No time to rest on your laurels. Let's move swiftly on to this next quiz . . .

1 Which of these birds does not migrate?
- ◆ Partridge
- ▲ Swallow
- ● Blackbird

2 What sense is essential for birds to navigate?
- ◆ Taste
- ▲ Touch
- ● Smell

3 True or false: Monarch butterflies rely on their antennae to tell them when to migrate.
- ◆ True
- ▲ False

4 Which tiny animal broke a record by flying from Russia to the French Alps?
- ◆ Butterfly
- ▲ Bat
- ● Pigeon
- ■ Robin

5 What fish leap up waterfalls as they travel upriver?
- ◆ Goldfish
- ▲ Salmon
- ● Trout

Did you know?

Arctic terns hold the record for the longest annual migration by any animal at 44,000 miles (70,800 km).

6 Which of these animals do not migrate?
◆ Wildebeest
▲ Dolphins
● Bats
■ Chimpanzees

7 What are molt migrant birds?
◆ Birds that migrate to shed their feathers
▲ Animals that love vinegar
● Birds that migrate towards treats

8 Why do birds living in the Amazon rainforest migrate less than birds in other habitats?
◆ They're lazy
▲ The weather is too hot for them to fly
● Weather and food supply are more reliable
■ Their wings are too small

9 How many miles does a caribou walk in a single year?
◆ Up to 250 miles (400 km)
▲ Over 500 miles (800 km)
● Over 2,000 miles (3,200 km)

10 True or false: Migrating turtles have a good sense of direction.
◆ True
▲ False

Turn to page 52 for the answers!

Migration
Answers

1 **Which of these birds does not migrate?**

◆ Partridge

Non migrating birds are called sedentary. A partridge stays in the same area for its entire lifetime.

2 **What sense is essential for birds to navigate?**

● Smell

Without their sense of smell, birds cannot navigate.

3 **True or false: Monarch butterflies rely on their antennae to tell them when to migrate.**

◆ True

The antennae have a genetic clock that tells them when to migrate. This is important as it's a new generation that migrates each year.

4 **Which tiny animal broke a record by flying from Russia to the French Alps?**

▲ Bat

A tiny bat flew 1,800 miles (2,900 km) over 63 days and set a new migration record.

5 **What fish leap up waterfalls as they travel upriver?**

▲ Salmon

Adult salmon live in the ocean, but travel upriver to fresh water to breed.

6 **Which of these animals do not migrate?**

■ Chimpanzees

Like humans, chimpanzees tend to stay in their troop's territory where they have established a community.

7 **What are molt migrant birds?**

◆ Birds that migrate to shed their feathers

Molt migrant birds, such as shelducks, lose all their flight feathers at once and cannot fly. They migrate to a safe spot before this happens.

8 **Why do birds living in the Amazon rainforest migrate less than birds in other habitats?**

● Weather and food supply are more reliable

The rainforest climate is hot and wet all year round, so birds' diets are not impacted by seasons in the same way.

9 **How many miles does a caribou walk in a single year?**

● Over 2,000 miles (3,200 km)

The Western Arctic caribou herd migrate this far in one year.

10 **True or false: Migrating turtles have a good sense of direction.**

▲ False

Turtles often seem to travel strange routes to reach their destination.

Podium!

Bronze: 1–5 correct answers

Silver: 6–8 correct answers

Gold: 9–10 correct answers

Rivers

Don't waste time worrying about your last score because you have bigger fish to fry now.

1 What river rodent has chisel-bladed teeth for chomping down trees?
- ◆ Beaver
- ▲ Salmon
- ● Otter
- ■ Water vole

2 Which of the below is a real-life river creature?
- ◆ Purple river leopard
- ▲ Pink river dolphin
- ● Green river seal
- ■ Blue river walrus

3 What is not from the mustelid family?
- ◆ Otter
- ▲ Kingfisher
- ● Badger
- ■ Mink

Did you know?
Some fish travel over 1,500 miles (2,500 km) to lay their eggs where they were born.

4 What do otters use their long whiskers for?
- ◆ Tickling predators
- ▲ Feeling prey
- ● As a disguise

5 True or false: The diving bell spider spends its life underwater in rivers.

◆ True

▲ False

6 How big is the average male American alligator?

◆ Up to 5 ft (1.5 m)

▲ Up to 10 ft (3 m)

● Up to 15 ft (4.5 m)

7 How many teeth can a crocodile have in its lifetime?

◆ Twenty

▲ Fifty

● Hundreds

■ Thousands

8 What is the main risk of frogs and toads laying eggs in rivers?

◆ Too many predators

▲ Not warm enough

● Not salty enough

■ The eggs could get washed away

9 How big can water snake litters be?

◆ Up to 10

▲ Up to 100

● More than 100

Scan the QR code for a Kahoot! about river animals.

Turn to page 56 for the answers!

10 Which of these is not a river fish?

◆ Sailfish

▲ Northern pike

● Salmon

Rivers Answers

2 **Which of the below is a real-life river creature?**

▲ Pink river dolphin

The males are pink. This is believed to be from scar tissue from rough games or fighting over females.

1 **What river rodent has chisel-bladed teeth for chomping down trees?**

◆ Beaver

Powerful teeth are needed for beavers to build their lodge, which is surrounded by a moat for extra protection.

3 **What is not from the mustelid family?**

▲ Kingfisher

A kingfisher is a bird. Mustelids are land animals that often hunt bigger animals, sometimes in water.

4 **What do otters use their long whiskers for?**

▲ Feeling prey

Swimming in murky waters means fish can be hard to find and hunt without super sensitive whiskers.

5 **True or false: The diving bell spider spends its life underwater in rivers.**

▲ False

The diving bell spider lives underwater in ponds and streams. Its underwater web looks like a diving bell.

6 **How big is the average male American alligator?**

● Up to 15 ft (4.5 m)

An alligator's tail makes up half of its length. Alligators can weigh up to 1,000 lb (half a tonne).

7 **How many teeth can a crocodile have in its lifetime?**

■ Thousands

As soon as a crocodile loses a tooth, a new one is ready to fill the gap.

9 **How big can water snake litters be?**

▲ Up to 100

Although 20 is more normal, up to 100 has been known for larger snakes.

8 **What is the main risk of frogs and toads laying eggs in rivers?**

■ The eggs could get washed away

Frogs and toads lay their eggs in reeds to keep them safely anchored until they hatch.

10 **Which of these is not a river fish?**

● Sailfish

These easily identifiable fish are found in the warmer waters of the Atlantic and Pacific oceans.

Podium!

Bronze: 1–5 correct answers
Silver: 6–8 correct answers
Gold: 9–10 correct answers

Wetlands

Let's hope this quiz about wetland animals doesn't leave you feeling out of your depth.

1 What do fishing cats like to eat?
- ◆ Fish, crabs, and frogs
- ▲ Weeds and plants
- ● Frogs eggs
- ■ Insects

2 What do mink do to show they're happy?
- ◆ Wag their tail
- ▲ Purr
- ● Puff up their fur
- ■ Dance

3 How do raccoons help support the ecosystem?
- ◆ By planting trees
- ▲ By promoting recycling
- ● By controlling rodent populations

4 Like all rattlesnakes, the massasauga rattlesnake that lives in wetland areas can sense heat. What does this help it to do?
- ◆ Sunbathe
- ▲ See prey in total darkness
- ● Predict the weather

Did you know?

Bald eagles aren't bald; the tops of their heads are white. They may get their name from the old English word "balde," which means white.

5 True or false: Antelopes have a split down the middle of their hooves.
- ◆ True
- ▲ False

6 Why does the male natterjack toad sing?
- ◆ To attract females
- ▲ In the hope of finding fame
- ● To entertain its friends

7 How many insects can a bat eat in one night?
- ◆ 100
- ▲ 200
- ● 3,000
- ■ 4,000

8 Which wetland insect has been around since prehistoric times?
- ◆ Ladybird
- ▲ Bumblebee
- ● Dragonfly

9 Why do curlews toss prey in the air, then catch and swallow it?
- ◆ Their tongues can't reach the prey
- ▲ For fun
- ● To impress other birds
- ■ To stun the prey

10 How do skunks keep unwanted wildlife away from them?
- ◆ By spraying
- ▲ By growling
- ● By vomiting

Turn to page 60 for the answers!

Wetlands Answers

1 **What do fishing cats like to eat?**

◆ Fish, crabs, and frogs

These water-loving cats are some of the best swimmers around with webbing on their feet. They mainly eat fish, but sometimes snack on crabs and frogs.

2 **What do mink do to show they're happy?**

▲ Purr

Like household cats, a mink purrs when it is content. When it is threatened, mink growl, hiss, or bark.

3 **How do raccoons help support the ecosystem?**

● By controlling rodent populations

They are seen as pests by many farmers, but raccoons prey upon rodents and keep the numbers under control.

4 Like all rattlesnakes, the massasauga rattlesnake that lives in wetland areas can sense heat. What does this help it to do?

▲ See prey in total darkness

It can detect prey's heat if the prey is warmer than its surroundings.

5 **True or false: Antelopes have a split down the middle of their hooves.**

◆ True

The hoof is divided into two toes. Lechwe live in swampy areas and have long, pointed hooves to help them walk through the water.

6 Why does the male natterjack toad sing?

◆ To attract females

This toad's loud croak can be heard up to 1.2 miles (2 km) away. In spring, they sing together to attract females.

7 How many insects can a bat eat in one night?

● 3,000

Bats wake not long after sunset and fly up to 33 ft (10 m) above the ground in search of food.

8 Which wetland insect has been around since prehistoric times?

● Dragonfly

These big-eyed insects have adapted since prehistoric times. Ancient versions of these wetland insects were the size of eagles!

9 Why do curlews toss prey in the air, then catch and swallow it?

◆ Their tongues can't reach the prey

Their down-curved bills are so long that their tongues can't reach the prey to flick it down into their mouth.

10 How do skunks keep unwanted wildlife away from them?

◆ By spraying

Skunks spray a harmful stink at any threat that comes near enough. The awful odor is hard to get rid of once it gets you.

Podium!
Bronze: 1–5 correct answers
Silver: 6–8 correct answers
Gold: 9–10 correct answers

Polar

Brrrr! It's cold out there. But this quiz will get your brain whirring and keep you warm!

1 What is the difference between animal life in the Arctic and the Antarctic?

◆ Many Arctic animals live on land, while most Antarctic animals live in the ocean

▲ Many Arctic animals live in the ocean, while most Antarctic animals live on land

2 How many krill are estimated to be in the Southern Ocean surrounding Antarctica?

◆ 2.2 million tons (2 million tonnes)

▲ 5.5 million tons (5 million tonnes)

● 11 million tons (10 million tonnes)

3 Which of these statements about the polar regions is incorrect?

◆ They have 24 hours of daylight in the summer and perpetual darkness in winter

▲ They are the coldest places on Earth

● They are all ice, snow, and rock

4 True or false: A breeding emperor penguin often has to walk 100 km (62 miles) or more across the ice to feed in open water.

◆ True

▲ False

5 How many members can a colony of Adélie penguins contain?

◆ Over a hundred

▲ Over a thousand

● Over a million

6 What likes to try to eat the crabeater seal?

◆ The polar bear

▲ The leopard seal

● The arctic fox

7 From how far away can a polar bear smell a seal on the ice?

◆ From more than 0.3 miles (0.5 km)

▲ From more than 0.6 miles (1 km)

● From more than 1.2 miles (2 km)

8 What can the temperature get down to before an Arctic fox is uncomfortable?

◆ -22°F (-30°C)

▲ -58°F (-50°C)

● -94°F (-70°C)

Scan the QR code for a Kahoot! about polar animals.

Turn to page 64 for the answers!

9 Put these Arctic animals in order of size from the biggest to the smallest.

◆ Arctic fox

▲ Polar bear

● Lemming

■ Walrus

Polar
Answers

1 What is the difference between animal life in the Arctic and the Antarctic?

◆ Many Arctic animals live on land, while most Antarctic animals live in the ocean

The Arctic has more animals living on the tundra, but the Antarctic is surrounded by ocean.

2 How many krill are estimated to be in the Southern Ocean surrounding Antarctica?

● 11 million tons

These small crustaceans that form the diet of seals and whales are in large enough groups to be seen by satellites in space.

3 Which of these statements about the polar regions is incorrect?

● They are all ice, snow, and rock

The Arctic has a multitude of plant life and many herbivores such as reindeer and Arctic hares visit to feed.

4 True or false: A breeding emperor penguin often has to walk 62 miles (100 km) or more across the ice to feed in open water.

◆ True

To survive the bitter Antarctic winter, while they wait for the return of the females, the male emperors form tight huddles of up to 5,000 birds.

5
How many members can a colony of Adélie penguins contain?

● Over a million

Only Adelie and emperor penguins spend winter in Antarctica.

6
What likes to try to eat the crabeater seal?

▲ The leopard seal

Up to 78 percent of crabeater seals have scars and injuries from failed leopard seal attacks.

7
From how far away can a polar bear smell a seal on the ice?

▲ From more than 0.6 miles (1 km)

The polar bear is the largest land predator and preys mainly on seals.

8
What can the temperature get down to before an Arctic fox is uncomfortable?

● -94°F (-70°C)

The Arctic fox has an amazing resistance to cold thanks to its extremely thick fur.

9
Put these Arctic animals in order of size from the biggest to the smallest.

▲ Polar bear
■ Walrus
◆ Arctic fox
● Lemming

Lemmings provide food for many Arctic animals, including foxes.

Podium!

Bronze: 1–4 correct answers
Silver: 5–7 correct answers
Gold: 8–9 correct answers

Grassland

Time to get into safari mode and get those binoculars out. You have questions to answer!

1 Why do many large plant-eaters live in herds?
- ◆ They like living with friends
- ▲ They aren't allowed to leave
- ● It increases their chances of survival

2 What is a group of lions called?
- ◆ A stride
- ▲ A pride
- ● A tribe

3 Which is the fastest?
- ◆ Ostrich
- ▲ Emu
- ● Cassowary
- ■ Rhea

4 True or false: No two giraffes have exactly the same coat pattern.
- ◆ True
- ▲ False

5
How much grass can a hippopotamus eat in one feeding?
- ◆ 106 lb (48 kg)
- ▲ 128 lb (58 kg)
- ● 150 lb (68 kg)

6
How many termites can inhabit a nest?
- ◆ Up to 3 million
- ▲ Up to 30 million
- ● Up to 300 million

7
Where do burrowing owls lay their eggs?
- ◆ In a nest
- ▲ Below the ground
- ● On the ground

8
How much more sensitive is the giant anteater's sense of smell than a human's?
- ◆ 40 times ▲ 50 times ● 60 times

Did you know?
Fires, ignited by lightning, are a natural feature of grassland life. But over time fires help grassland wildlife.

9
Which of these is not from the bovid species?
- ◆ Bison
- ▲ Warthog
- ● Antelope
- ■ Gazelle

10
How do dung beetles use dung?
- ◆ They roll it into balls to play with
- ▲ They roll it into balls to feed their grubs
- ● They roll it into balls and live in it

Turn to page 68 for the answers!

Grassland
Answers

1 **Why do many large plant-eaters live in herds?**

● It increases their chances of survival

It's more difficult for predators to attack, because while most members of the herd are eating, some look out for danger.

2 **What is a group of lions called?**

▲ A pride

A pride consists of up to eight adult females, their young, and between one and three adult males.

3 **Which is the fastest?**

◆ Ostrich

At full stretch, an ostrich can run at 43 mph (70 kph). That's as fast as a racehorse.

4 **True or false: No two giraffes have exactly the same coat pattern.**

◆ True

Each species has its own distinct pattern—they are all subtly different.

5 How much grass can a hippopotamus eat in one feeding?

● 150 lb (68 kg)

They emerge at night to graze on land for up to five hours.

6 How many termites can inhabit a nest?

▲ Up to 30 million

These accomplished builders construct giant, elaborate, subterranean nests that extend high above ground level.

7 Where do burrowing owls lay their eggs?

▲ Below the ground

They do this because there are no trees to make nest holes in.

8 How much more sensitive is the giant anteater's sense of smell than a human's?

◆ 40 times

Anteaters use smell to identify species of ant.

9 Which of these is not from the bovid species?

▲ Warthog

Bovids are two-toed hoofed animals. Unlike most pigs, warthogs spend the night in underground burrows.

10 How do dung beetles use dung?

▲ They roll it into balls to feed their grubs

They then bury the dung balls underground.

Podium!

Bronze: 1–5 correct answers
Silver: 6–8 correct answers
Gold: 9–10 correct answers

Farmyard

So you know your pigs from your sheep. Get a moo-ve on and find out whether you know your barnyard animals in this quiz.

1 Which were farmed first?
◆ Sheep and goats
▲ Cattle

2 What process is responsible for all domesticated animals?
◆ Natural selection
▲ Artificial selection
● Random selection

3 What animal are donkeys related to?
◆ Horses
▲ Asses
● Cows

4 What process do cows do after swallowing their food?
◆ They bring it up and spit it out
▲ They bring it up to chew and swallow it again

Did you know?
The chicken is the closest living relative to the T. Rex. There are similarities in their anatomy!

5 How many piglets does the average pig give birth to?
◆ 10–11
▲ 17–19
● 20–21

6 Which animal's milk is not used for human consumption?
◆ Cow
▲ Pig
● Sheep
■ Yak

7 What animal is used to herd farm animals?
◆ Dog
▲ Cat
● Chicken

8 True or false: A chicken has body parts called a comb, a brush, and a mirror.
◆ True
▲ False

9 How many stomach compartments does a sheep have?
◆ Two
▲ Four
● Six

Scan the QR code for a Kahoot! about farmyard animals.

10 Which farm animal weighs the most?
◆ A bull
▲ A boar
● A stallion

Turn to page 72 for the answers!

Farmyard Answers

1 **Which were farmed first?**

◆ Sheep and goats

They were probably domesticated 8,000–9,000 years ago, in southwest Asia. Cattle were domesticated about 2,000 years later (also in southwest Asia).

2 **What process is responsible for all domesticated animals?**

▲ Artificial selection

Artificial selection is when humans breed animals to ensure that they have specific characteristics.

3 **What animal are donkeys related to?**

▲ Asses

Donkeys are descendants of the African wild ass. They are now used around the world as working animals.

4 **What process do cows do after swallowing their food?**

▲ They bring it up to chew and swallow it again

This process is called chewing the cud. It helps cattle to digest tough plants.

5 **How many piglets does the average pig give birth to?**

◆ 10–11

A female pig gives birth after a pregnancy of about four months.

6 Which animal's milk is not used for human consumption?

▲ Pig

Pigs are considered too difficult to milk, although it is possible for humans to drink their milk.

7 What animal is used to herd farm animals?

◆ Dog

Sheepdogs are bred to herd animals. The border collie is one of the most intelligent dogs in the world!

8 True or false: A chicken has body parts called a comb, a brush, and a mirror.

▲ False

But the skin that sticks up from the top of the head is called a comb.

9 How many stomach compartments does a sheep have?

▲ Four

They regurgitate their food (bring it back up from the stomach) and chew it again. This helps them fully digest the food.

10 Which farm animal weighs the most?

◆ A bull

A bull can weigh up to 4,000 lb (1,800 kg). The largest pig in history weighed 2,552 lb (1,157 kg).

Podium!

Bronze: 1–5 correct answers

Silver: 6–8 correct answers

Gold: 9–10 correct answers

Nocturnal

Are you a night owl? Then this quiz will be right up your moonlit street!

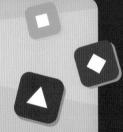

1 Which of these animals is not nocturnal?
- ◆ Bat
- ▲ Owl
- ● Tiger

2 What animal has been spotted with the honey badger, breaking into bees nests?
- ◆ The greater honeyguide bird
- ▲ The lesser honeyspot bird
- ● The medium honeylife bird

3 True or false: An owl's eyes are fixed in place and it cannot roll them to look at something.
- ◆ True
- ▲ False

4 The luna moth has a very short lifespan. How long does it live for?
- ◆ A week
- ▲ A fortnight
- ● A month

5 Where is the platypus during the day?
- ◆ It looks for food in the water
- ▲ It remains inside its burrow
- ● It rests on the riverbank

6 How far can the sugar glider fly?
- ◆ 98 ft (30 m)
- ▲ 131 ft (40 m)
- ● 164 ft (50 m)

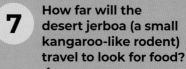

7 How far will the desert jerboa (a small kangaroo-like rodent) travel to look for food?
- ◆ 3 miles (5 km)
- ▲ 6 miles (10 km)
- ● 9 miles (15 km)

Did you know?
The male nightingale sings both by day and by night. It uses its daytime songs to mark its territory and its nocturnal songs to attract females.

8 Tarantulas are nocturnal hunters. What wouldn't they catch as prey from this list?
- ◆ Frogs
- ▲ Lizards
- ● Birds
- ■ Skunks

9 Why is the aye-aye known as a nighttime "woodpecker?"
- ◆ It taps trees with its long middle finger as it looks for grubs
- ▲ It knocks on trees with its nose as it searches for insects
- ● It uses its large ears to listen for knocking noises of insects

10 How do bats navigate in the dark?
- ◆ Using echolocation
- ▲ Using echonavigation
- ● Using echomaps

Turn to page 76 for the answers!

Nocturnal Answers

1 Which of these animals is not nocturnal?

● Tiger

Tigers are active at dawn and dusk, this is called being crepuscular.

2 What animal has been spotted with the honey badger, breaking into bees nests?

◆ The greater honeyguide bird

The bird leads the badger to bee nests. The badger opens the nest for them both.

3 True or false: An owl's eyes are fixed in place and it cannot roll them to look at something.

◆ True

Luckily, an owl's neck enables it to swivel its head up to 270 degrees, which is three-quarters of a full turn.

4 The luna moth has a very short lifespan. How long does it live for?

◆ A week

During the day they rest in dark crevices on trees.

5 Where is the platypus during the day?

▲ It remains inside its burrow

It emerges at night to search the muddy bottom of shallow pools for food.

6 How far can the sugar glider fly?

● 164 ft (50 m)

This small nocturnal marsupial can glide from tree to tree on a furry membrane of skin stretched between its limbs.

7 How far will the desert jerboa (a small kangaroo-like rodent) travel to look for food?

▲ 6 miles (10 km)

They are entirely nocturnal, and feed mainly on seeds. They travel by hopping on their long back legs and balancing with their tails.

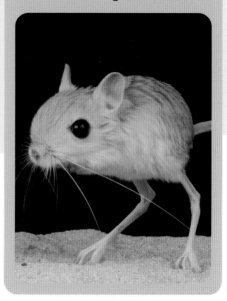

8 Tarantulas are nocturnal hunters. What wouldn't they catch as prey from this list?

■ Skunks

Skunks will try to dig tarantulas out of their burrows!

9 Why is the aye-aye known as a nighttime "woodpecker?"

◆ It taps trees with its long middle finger as it looks for grubs

The aye-aye was thought to be extinct until its rediscovery in Madagsascar in 1957.

10 How do bats navigate in the dark?

◆ Using echolocation

A bat can detect a flying moth from up to 19.5 ft (6 m) away.

Podium!

Bronze: 1–5 correct answers
Silver: 6–8 correct answers
Gold: 9–10 correct answers

Animal Babies

Is there anything as cute as a little baby? Maybe this animal baby quiz!

1 How long will a baby humpback whale swim with its mother?
◆ At least six months
▲ At least a year
● At least 18 months

2 How often can female hamsters have babies?
◆ Once a month
▲ Once a year
● Every five years

4 What is the process of a tadpole turning into a frog called?
◆ Camouflage
▲ Evolution
● Metamorphosis
■ Gestation

3 Where do dragonflies lay their eggs?
◆ In the water
▲ On a leaf
● On reeds

Did you know?
The weight of a single ostrich egg is 3 lb (1.4 kg). That's heavier than at least 20 hen's eggs!

5 How long will a Californian sea lion stay with its newborn pup?

◆ About seven days

▲ About three days

● About a day

6 Where does the American burying beetle lay her eggs?

◆ On dead bodies of animals

▲ Under the ground

● In a nest

■ Up a tree

7 How often can a female orangutan have a baby?

◆ Every 2.5 years

▲ Every 4.7 years

● Every 9.3 years

8 How many eggs can a sea lamprey lay at one time?

◆ 10,000

▲ 100,000

● 1,000,000

9 Which of these have fully formed babies born to them?

◆ Scorpion

▲ Platypus

● Kangaroo

10 True or false: The female seahorse gives birth to baby seahorses.

◆ True

▲ False

Scan the QR code for a Kahoot! about animal babies.

Turn to page 80 for the answers!

Animal Babies
Answers

1 **How long will a baby humpback whale swim with its mother?**

▲ At least a year

Fully grown they can weigh up to 37 tons (34 tonnes).

2 **How often can female hamsters have babies?**

◆ Once a month

They can have babies at about two months old. A litter has between one and 13 babies.

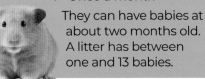

3 **Where do dragonflies lay their eggs?**

◆ In the water

They hatch as aquatic nymphs and grow for two or three years in the water.

4 **What is the process of a tadpole turning into a frog called?**

● Metamorphosis

A frog egg develops into a long-tailed tadpole. It grows legs, and turns into a tiny air-breathing froglet. Its tail shrinks away and it hops onto land to begin adult life.

5 **How long will a Californian sea lion stay with its newborn pup?**

◆ About seven days

It then leaves the pup for three days to go hunting for food.

6 **Where does the American burying beetle lay her eggs?**

◆ On dead bodies of animals

The bodies provide food for when babies hatch.

7 **How often can a female orangutan have a baby?**

● Every 9.3 years

Orangutans can live for up to 58 years in the wild.

8 **How many eggs can a sea lamprey lay at one time?**

▲ 100,000

It looks like an eel but it is actually a jawless fish.

9 **Which of these have fully formed babies born to them?**

◆ Scorpion

Scorpion babies are born fully developed, whereas the female red kangaroo produces a tiny, blind, naked creature that is little more than an embryo. A platypus is one of the few mammals to lay eggs.

10 **True or false: The female seahorse gives birth to baby seahorses.**

▲ False

Males give birth. Females deposit hundreds of eggs in the male's pouch. Male spotted seahorses often give birth at night during a full moon.

Podium!

Bronze: 1–5 correct answers

Silver: 6–8 correct answers

Gold: 9–10 correct answers

Hibernating

Animals that hibernate spend the winter in a long, deep sleep. Don't fall asleep while trying these questions!

1 **What happens when animals hibernate?**
◆ Everything slows down
▲ Everything speeds up
● They just go to sleep

2 **Which of these animals hibernate in large groups?**
◆ Bats
▲ Hedgehogs
● Dormice

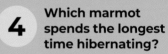

Did you know?
Fully grown ladybugs hibernate during the winter, often in large groups.

4 **Which marmot spends the longest time hibernating?**
◆ Yellow-bellied marmot
▲ Alpine marmot

3 **What is an important part of hibernation for a hedgehog?**
◆ Food stores
▲ Water sources
● Camouflage
■ Exercise

5 How do animals prepare for hibernation?
- ◆ They eat more
- ▲ They eat less
- ● They eat the same
- ■ They don't eat

6 Which of these geckos hibernates?
- ◆ The common leopard gecko
- ▲ The Moorish gecko
- ● Both of them do

7 How long will the hazel dormouse hibernate for?
- ◆ About 3 months
- ▲ About 5 months
- ● About 7 months

8 Where do garter snakes hibernate in huge numbers?
- ◆ The fringes of the Arctic
- ▲ The edges of Antarctica

10 True or false: The American black bear doesn't truly hibernate—it sleeps.
- ◆ True
- ▲ False

Turn to page 84 for the answers!

9 When will tortoises hibernate?
- ◆ When it's very cool
- ▲ When they are bored
- ● When they don't have enough food

Hibernating
Answers

1 **What happens when animals hibernate?**
- ◆ Everything slows down

Their temperature and heart rate fall, their breathing slows, and they draw on stored fat reserves.

2 **Which of these animals hibernate in large groups?**
- ◆ Bats

Bats that hibernate in large colonies lose less fat energy than those that hibernate solo.

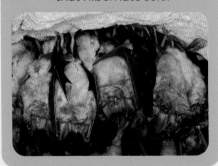

3 **What is an important part of hibernation for a hedgehog?**
- ● Camouflage

Hedgehogs gather piles of leaves to hide in during hibernation.

4 **Which marmot spends the longest time hibernating?**
- ◆ Yellow-bellied marmot

It spends up to eight months in hibernation. The Alpine marmot spends up to half the year.

5 **How do animals prepare for hibernation?**
- ◆ They eat more

They store fat to keep them alive during the months when they do not eat. Some hibernators collect and store food before hibernating.

6 Which of these geckos hibernates?

● Both of them do

The common leopard gecko may also aestivate. This is when an animal goes into a similar state to hibernation, but during the summer.

7 How long will the hazel dormouse hibernate for?

● About 7 months

"Dor" from its name means "sleeping"!

8 Where do garter snakes hibernate in huge numbers?

◆ The fringes of the Arctic

There is a real spectacle when large numbers of snakes emerge in spring.

9 When will tortoises hibernate?

◆ When it's very cool

The leopard tortoise lives in a range of habitats and may bury itself to hibernate when cooler.

10 True or false: The American black bear doesn't truly hibernate—it sleeps.

◆ True

Its body temperature drops only a few degrees so it can wake up more easily.

Podium!

Bronze: 1–5 correct answers
Silver: 6–8 correct answers
Gold: 9–10 correct answers

Flippers and Fins

Do you know your lionfish from your lamprey and your sailfish from your sea turtle?

1 Which of the following terms best describes the green sea turtle?
- ◆ Carnivore
- ▲ Herbivore
- ● Omnivore

2 How do lionfish herd their prey?
- ◆ They use their wide mouths to push them along
- ▲ They use their long pectoral fins
- ● They use their head tentacles to mesmerize them
- ■ They make a whistling sound

3 True or false: Almost all species of fish have a skeleton made of cartilage.
- ◆ True
- ▲ False

4 How long is the giant manta ray?
- ◆ Up to 11 ft (3.4 m)
- ▲ Up to 17 ft (5.2 m)
- ● Up to 25 ft (7.6 m)

5 True or false: A sailfish was once recorded leaping from the water at 68 mph (110 kph).
◆ True
▲ False

Did you know?
Sharks can track prey using sensors, which detect electrical signals generated by an animal's muscles.

6 Which of these is the longest?
◆ Leatherback turtle
▲ Atlantic cod
● Angel shark

7 Who owns these teeth?
◆ Great white shark
▲ Sea lamprey
● Green moray eel

8 Put these sharks in order of size:
◆ Scalloped hammerhead
▲ Basking shark
● Whale shark

9 When did the earliest bony fish live?
◆ 110 million years ago
▲ 230 million years ago
● 420 million years ago

Scan the QR code for a Kahoot! about animals with flippers.

10 Do fish have ears?
◆ No
▲ Yes

Turn to page 88 for the answers!

Flippers and Fins

Answers

1 Which of the following terms best describes the green sea turtle?

▲ Herbivore

Most turtles are carnivorous but these are herbivores, feeding mainly on seagrasses and marine algae.

2 How do lionfish herd their prey?

▲ They use their long pectoral fins

Lionfish herd prey into tight corners where they are easier to catch. Their head tentacles act as lures.

3 True or false: Almost all species of fish have a skeleton made of cartilage.

▲ False

There are only 1,200 species of cartilaginous fish. They have skeletons made from gristly, pliable cartilage instead of bone.

4 How long is the giant manta ray?

● Up to 25 ft (7.6 m)

The biggest of the rays, giant manta rays are filter feeders like basking sharks.

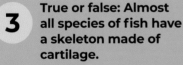

5 **True or false: A sailfish was once recorded leaping from the water at 68 mph (110 kph).**
◆ True
It's the fastest fish in the sea, able to outpace a powerful speedboat.

6 **Which of these is the longest?**
◆ Leatherback turtle
It's up to 8.8 ft (2.7 m) and is the biggest turtle. Atlantic cod grow up to up to 6.5 ft (2 m), while angel sharks reach up to 7.8 ft (2.4 m).

7 **Who owns these teeth?**
◆ Great white shark
A sea lamprey has a sucker armed with rows of sharp teeth. Morays have sharp hooked teeth.

8 **Put these sharks in order of size.**
● Whale shark—41 ft (12.5 m) long or more
▲ Basking shark—up to 33 ft (10 m) long
◆ Scalloped hammerhead—up to 13.8 ft (4.2 m) long

9 **When did the earliest bony fish live?**
● 420 million years ago
Jawless fish (cartilage skeletons) were first to evolve so are even older!

Podium!
Bronze: 1–5 correct answers
Silver: 6–8 correct answers
Gold: 9–10 correct answers

10 **Do fish have ears?**
◆ No
But they can sense sound waves and, more importantly, they detect pressure changes using a network of sensors called the lateral line.

Insects

Are you up on all things creepy and crawly? See if you can find all the right ant-sers!

1 Which is the heaviest beetle in the world?

◆ Goliath beetle
▲ Stag beetle
● Great diving beetle

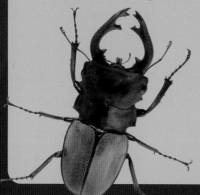

2 What is the largest known butterfly in the world?

◆ Queen Alexandra's birdwing
▲ Painted lady
● Monarch

4 How many lenses are there in a dragonfly's eye?

◆ 10,000
▲ 20,000
● 30,000

3 How many known species of beetle are there?

◆ 37,000
▲ 370,000
● 3,700,000

5 True or false: All moths only come out at night.
- ◆ True
- ▲ False

6 How many times do locusts shed their skins?
- ◆ 3
- ▲ 4
- ● 5

7 What are the most deadly animals on Earth?
- ◆ Wasps
- ▲ Mosquitoes
- ● Sharks

8 What makes a bee buzz?
- ◆ Its furry body
- ▲ Its sensitive antennae
- ● Its wings beating

9 Which of these are not from the arthropod family?
- ◆ Insects
- ▲ Crustaceans
- ● Mollusks
- ■ Arachnids

10 What are insects?
- ◆ Invertebrates
- ▲ Vertebrates

Did you know?
Scientists estimate that up to 90 percent of all species of animals in the world are insects.

Turn to page 92 for the answers!

Insects
Answers

1 Which is the heaviest beetle in the world?
◆ Goliath beetle
It can weigh up to 3.5 oz (100 g).

2 What is the largest known butterfly in the world?
◆ Queen Alexandra's birdwing
It has a wingspan of up to 10.8 in (30 cm) and is only found in certain forests in part of Papua New Guinea.

3 How many known species of beetle are there?
▲ 370,000
Almost a quarter of all known animal species are beetles.

4 How many lenses are there in a dragonfly's eye?
● 30,000
Humans only have one lens in each eye.

5 True or false: All moths only come out at night.
▲ False
Several different moths come out in the day, including hummingbird hawkmoths. They hover over flowers sipping nectar, like their tropical bird namesake.

6 How many times do locusts shed their skins?

● 5

They shed these skins as they grow. The locusts' tough skins act as external skeletons.

7 What are the most deadly animals on Earth?

▲ Mosquitoes

The parasites that they carry in their bodies are responsible for at least a million human deaths every year.

8 What makes a bee buzz?

● Its wings beating

A bee's wings beat 250 times per second.

9 Which of these are not from the arthropod family?

● Mollusks

More than 80 percent of all known animal species are arthropods. Most of them are insects.

10 What are insects?

◆ Invertebrates

An invertebrate is any animal that does not have an internal jointed skeleton.

Podium!

Bronze: 1–5 correct answers

Silver: 6–8 correct answers

Gold: 9–10 correct answers

Camouflage

Unlike the creatures in this quiz, who are masters of the art, you can't hide from these questions!

1 Which animal changes its coat from brownish gray in the summer to white in the autumn?

◆ Leopard seal

▲ Emperor penguin

● Arctic fox

2 What's in this picture?

◆ A frog

▲ A leaf insect

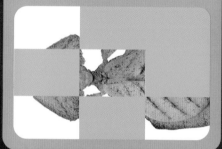

3 Chameleons are well-known for their camouflage abilities, but what else can some of them do?

◆ Change their body shape entirely into a snake

▲ Extend their tongue to twice their body length to seize prey

● Bark like a dog

4 How does a snow leopard stay camouflaged?

◆ It hides among trees and bushes

▲ It hides among rocks and lichen

● It hides in dark caves

5 What is unusual about the glasswing butterfly's camouflage?

◆ It's wings are made of glass

▲ The middle of each wing is transparent

● It's completely invisible

6 Which shark uses camouflage to ambush prey?
- ◆ Angel shark
- ▲ Thresher shark
- ● Hammerhead shark

7 Which of these animals has effective camouflage for long grass?
- ◆ Giraffe
- ▲ Tiger
- ● Elephant

8 How do desert spiders use camouflage?
- ◆ By sticking sand to themselves
- ▲ By wearing shells
- ● By changing color

Did you know?
Cuttlefish can change their color and pattern to match their surroundings.

9 How does the long-nosed horn frog camouflage itself?
- ◆ It looks like tree bark
- ▲ It looks like dead leaves
- ● It looks like a tropical flower

Scan the QR code for a Kahoot! about animal camouflage.

10 True or false: Crocodiles climb low trees to hide.
- ◆ True
- ▲ False

Turn to page 96 for the answers!

Camouflage
Answers

1 Which animal changes its coat from brownish gray in the summer to white in the autumn?

● Arctic fox

In the treeless Arctic tundra, camouflage is one of the most effective ways of both avoiding attack and of making an attack unseen.

2 What's in this picture?

▲ A leaf insect

These insects mimic real leaves swaying gently in the breeze.

4 How does a snow leopard stay camouflaged?

▲ It hides among rocks and lichen

Even in daylight it can be difficult to spot when it is sitting on a boulder.

3 Chameleons are well-known for their camouflage abilities, but what else can some of them do?

▲ Extend their tongue to twice their body length to seize prey

The tongue is curled up in the mouth when it's not in use, and it has a sticky tip that catches the prey.

5 What is unusual about the glasswing butterfly's camouflage?

▲ The middle of each wing is transparent

This allows the butterfly to blend in with its surroundings.

6 Which shark uses camouflage to ambush prey?

◆ Angel shark

Its ray-like shape enables it to hide on the sea bed.

7 Which of these animals has effective camouflage for long grass?

▲ Tiger

Their stripes mimic the vertical pattern of light and shade, and break up the tiger's outline, allowing it to get close to its target.

8 How do desert spiders use camouflage?

◆ By sticking sand to themselves

They attach sand to their upper bodies to blend in with their sandy habitat.

9 How does the long-nosed horn frog camouflage itself?

▲ It looks like dead leaves

It's almost invisible on the tropical forest floor, so can easily ambush small animal prey.

10 True or false: Crocodiles climb low trees to hide.

◆ True

Crocodiles can be found hiding in plain sight on branches over water as they wait to ambush prey.

Podium!

Bronze: 1–5 correct answers
Silver: 6–8 correct answers
Gold: 9–10 correct answers

Rodents

Don't be scared of mice and their cousins – see how much you know about them instead!

1 Which is the biggest rodent?
- ◆ Capybara
- ▲ Prairie dog
- ● Crested porcupine

2 What proportion of all mammal species are rodents?
- ◆ Quarter
- ▲ Third
- ● Half

3 How far can the spotted giant flying squirrel glide?
- ◆ More than 1,300 ft (400 m)
- ▲ More than 2,000 ft (600 m)
- ● More than 2,600 ft (800 m)

4 Where would you find a naked mole rat?
- ◆ South America
- ▲ Eastern Africa
- ● Europe

5 What are prairie dog burrow systems known as?
- ◆ Prairie dog towns
- ▲ Prairie dog cities
- ● Prairie dog villages

6 Why do Norway lemmings make mass migrations?

◆ Because they like traveling

▲ To avoid predators

● Because of food shortages

Did you know?
Rodents are found worldwide in every habitat apart from Antarctica.

7 True or false: Lions have been known to die of wounds inflicted by the quills of porcupines they have attacked.

◆ True

▲ False

8 How high will a beaver build a dam?

◆ 6.5 ft (2 m)

▲ 13 ft (4 m)

● 20 ft (6 m)

9 Which rodent killed nearly half of Europe's population in the 14th century?

◆ Hazel dormouse

▲ Red squirrel

● Black rat

10 How far can a South African springhare leap in a single bound?

◆ 3.25 ft (1 m)

▲ 6.5 ft (2 m)

● 10 ft (3 m)

Turn to page 100 for the answers!

Rodents
Answers

1 **Which is the biggest rodent?**

◆ Capybara

They grow up to 4.25 ft (1.3 m) long. Prairie dogs grow up to 15 in (38 cm) long and crested porcupines grow up to 3.25 ft (1 m) long.

2 **What proportion of all mammal species are rodents?**

● Half

Rodents are mostly small, plant-eating animals such as mice and squirrels. They all have big, self-sharpening front teeth for gnawing tough foods.

3 **How far can the spotted giant flying squirrel glide?**

◆ More than 1,300 ft (400 m)

They generally glide from high in one tree to lower in another rather than to the ground. They often glide to escape danger.

4 **Where would you find a naked mole rat?**

▲ Eastern Africa

This rodent lives in a colony controlled by a single breeding queen, rather like a colony of honeybees.

5 **What are prairie dog burrow systems known as?**

◆ Prairie dog towns

Prairie dogs are not dogs but ground squirrels. The biggest prairie dog town ever found was home to 400 million prairie dogs.

6 Why do Norway lemmings make mass migrations?

● Because of food shortages

This Arctic species is a prolific breeder and may produce so many young in a good year that food shortages can occur.

7 True or false: Lions have been known to die of wounds inflicted by the quills of porcupines they have attacked.

◆ True

When threatened, the porcupine charges tailfirst and embeds its sharp quills in its attacker's skin.

9 Which rodent killed nearly half of Europe's population in the 14th century?

● Black rat

Along with some other species, the black rat accidentally spread the bubonic plague around the world by traveling on ships.

8 How high will a beaver build a dam?

▲ 13 ft (4 m)

The longest-known beaver dam extended for 2,790 ft (850m).

Podium!

Bronze: 1–5 correct answers

Silver: 6–8 correct answers

Gold: 9–10 correct answers

10 How far can a South African springhare leap in a single bound?

▲ 6.5 ft (2 m)

It's not a hare, but a rodent and it can leap like a kangaroo on its long hind legs, balanced by its long, bushy tail.

Shelled

Don't be shy and hide under that shell. Come out and do this quiz!

1 What is the purpose of a shell?
- ◆ To protect a creature's body
- ▲ To anchor a creature to the ocean floor
- ● To keep the creature warm

2 Which is the heaviest living mollusk?
- ◆ Swan mussel
- ▲ Giant clam
- ● Queen conch

Did you know?
Horseshoe crabs, also known as king crabs, are not crustaceans but close relatives of spiders.

3 True or false: No bivalves can swim.
- ◆ True
- ▲ False

4 A very old edible clam was found in the North Atlantic in 2006. How old was it?
- ◆ 307 years old
- ▲ 507 years old
- ● 707 years old

5 True or false: Oysters cement themselves directly onto a surface such as a rock or shell?

◆ True
◆ False

6 What does it mean if a creature has a bivalve shell?

◆ It has a shell with two halves
▲ It can blow bubbles from it's shell
● It can't open it's shell

7 What are barnacles relatives of?

◆ Shrimps
▲ Sea slugs
● Cockles

8 Which snail has venom powerful enough to kill a human?

◆ Textile cone snail
▲ Red ramshorn snail
● Garden snail

9 How big is the largest-known crustacean, the Japanese spider crab?

◆ Up to 6.5 ft (2 m)
▲ Up to 13 ft (4 m)
● Up to 19.6 ft (6 m)

Scan the QR code for a Kahoot! about shelled creatures.

10 How do mussels hang onto rocks?

◆ They use a sticky, glue-like substance
▲ They insert their shells into cracks on the rocks
● They use strong, silk-like threads

Turn to page 104 for the answers!

Shelled Answers

1 What is the purpose of a shell?

◆ To protect a creature's body

Shells offer creatures protection from predators as they can pull their body inside it.

2 Which is the heaviest living mollusk?

▲ Giant clam

The giant clam has a shell measuring up to 4.5 ft (1.4 m) across. A swan mussel grows up to 9 in (23 cm) across and a queen conch grows up to 13.75 in (35 cm).

3 True or false: No bivalves can swim.

▲ False

Scallops swim by clapping their hinged shells together to force water out and shoot themselves backward out of danger.

4 A very old edible clam was found in the North Atlantic in 2006. How old was it?

▲ 507 years old

It was the oldest-known living animal.

5 True or false: Oysters cement themselves directly onto a surface such as a rock or shell?

◆ True

The edible oyster cements its left-hand valve onto a surface and then lives lying on its side. Oysters have been a valued food source since prehistoric times.

6 What does it mean if a creature has a bivalve shell?

◆ It has a shell with two halves

They are joined along one edge by elastic material and closed by contracting the adductor muscles.

7 What are barnacles relatives of?

◆ Shrimps

When barnacles are mature they settle on rocks, grow shells, and gather food with their feathery limbs.

8 Which snail has venom powerful enough to kill a human?

◆ Textile cone snail

The beautifully marked shell of this tropical sea snail conceals a deadly weapon—a tiny harpoon that injects a potent nerve poison.

9 How big is the largest-known crustacean, the Japanese spider crab?

▲ Up to 13 ft (4 m)

The Japanese spider crab has huge claws that can span up to 13 ft (4 m).

Podium!

Bronze: 1–5 correct answers
Silver: 6–8 correct answers
Gold: 9–10 correct answers

10 How do mussels hang onto rocks?

● They use strong, silk-like threads

The threads allow mussels to stay put even when there are powerful currents or waves.

Famous Animals

There are many well-known people in the world, but how much do you know about famous animals?

1 Which of these characters was based on an animal who lived at London Zoo?
- ◆ Bambi
- ▲ Mickey Mouse
- ● Winnie the Pooh
- ■ Kermit the Frog

2 What was the name of the first monkey in space?
- ◆ Ham the chimp
- ▲ Pam the baboon
- ● Tam the orangutan

3 How long ago did the dinosaurs live?
- ◆ 45.3 million years ago
- ▲ 55.2 million years ago
- ● 65.5 million years ago

4 When did dodos become extinct?
- ◆ 1600s
- ▲ 1700s
- ● 1800s

5 How many shipwrecks did Sam the cat manage to survive in WWII?

◆ 1
▲ 2
● 3

6 What was homing pigeon Cher Ami's famous mission in World War I?

◆ Flying 25 miles in 25 minutes to save a battalion
▲ Doing an aerial display to cheer up the troops

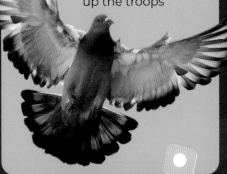

7 In her book *Born Free* what animal does the author Joy Adamson write about?

◆ Elsa the lioness
▲ Edna the tiger
● Edith the leopard

8 What type of animal is Punxsutawney Phil?

◆ A groundhog, or woodchuck
▲ A rat
● A chinchilla

9 Which country launched the rocket that sent Laika the dog into space?

◆ China
▲ USA
● Russia

10 True or false: In 1996, Dolly the sheep became the first successfully cloned mammal from an adult cell.

◆ True
▲ False

Did you know?

The tiger shark preserved as art in 1991 by artist Damien Hirst was worth US$62,550 (£50,000)

Turn to page 108 for the answers!

Famous Animals

Answers

1 **Which of these characters was based on an animal who lived at London Zoo?**
● Winnie the Pooh
Winnipeg was an American black bear and was visited by author A. A. Milne.

2 **What was the name of the first monkey in space?**
◆ Ham the chimp
His journey into space on January 31, 1961 was short, but he traveled 250 km (155 miles) in 16.5 minutes.

3 **How long ago did the dinosaurs live?**
● 65.5 million years ago
Dinosaurs were the main animals on Earth for more than 150 million years.

4 **When did dodos become extinct?**
◆ 1600s
Dodos lived on Mauritius, an island in the Indian Ocean. Humans arrived in about 1507 and began to hunt dodos.

5 **How many shipwrecks did Sam the cat manage to survive in WWII?**
● 3
He survived the sinking of the Bismarck in 1941, then the HMS Cossack, and finally the HMS Ark Royal.

6 What was homing pigeon Cher Ami's famous mission in World War I?

◆ Flying 25 miles in 25 minutes to save a battalion

Homing pigeons were a huge part of battlefield communication. This famous mission saved a battalion of American soldiers in France.

7 In her book *Born Free* what animal does the author Joy Adamson write about?

◆ Elsa the lioness

She lived like a domesticated pet, but was gradually reintroduced to life in the wild.

8 What type of animal is Punxsutawney Phil?

◆ A groundhog, or woodchuck

Phil has been predicting the weather in Pennsylvania, USA, since the 1800s. Seeing a woodchuck early in the year is a traditional sign that spring is not far off.

9 Which country launched the rocket that sent Laika the dog into space?

● Russia

She was the first ever dog in space, but sadly she died on the journey.

10 True or false: In 1996, Dolly the sheep became the first successfully cloned mammal from an adult cell.

◆ True

Dolly was grown from a single mammary cell that contained all the information to create a whole new sheep.

Podium!

Bronze: 1–4 correct answers

Silver: 5–7 correct answers

Gold: 8–9 correct answers

Birds

Don't get in a flap! There are over 10,000 species of birds, but how much do you know about them?

1 Almost half of the birds in the world belong to which group?
- ◆ Passerines, or perching birds
- ▲ Birds of prey
- ● Owls
- ■ Parrots

2 What job does the bird's bill pictured help with?
- ◆ Cracking nuts
- ▲ Probing mud
- ● Gathering nectar
- ■ Fighting

Did you know?
Birds are toothless, so they have an organ called a gizzard to grind up food.

3 True or false: The biggest bird in the world can't fly.
- ◆ True
- ▲ False

4 What bird likes to impale its prey on thorns to save and eat later?
- ◆ Red-backed shrike
- ▲ Hawk
- ● Raven

5 Which of these is a male turkey's call?
◆ Gobbling
▲ Cawing
● Hooting
■ Screeching

6 How big is the wingspan of the wandering albatross?
◆ 5 ft (1.5 m)
▲ 8 ft (2.5 m)
● 11 ft (3.5 m)

7 What bird is also called the American eagle?
◆ Bald eagle
▲ Golden eagle
● Harpy eagle

8 How can cassowaries cause severe injury?
◆ With their bills
▲ With their wings
● With their feet

9 How many fish can an Atlantic puffin carry in its bill?
◆ Up to 10
▲ Up to 20
● Up to 30

10 How many starlings might gather to roost for the night in the winter?
◆ 150
▲ 1,500
● 1.5 million

Scan the QR code for a Kahoot! about birds.

Turn to page 112 for the answers!

Birds
Answers

1 **Almost half of the birds in the world belong to which group?**

◆ Passerines, or perching birds

They share an ability to perch on the most slender twigs, and include all the most musical songbirds.

2 **What job does the bird's bill pictured help with?**

▲ Probing mud

Birds such as curlews have long, sensitive bills for probing into soft mud in search of prey.

3 **True or false: The biggest bird in the world can't fly.**

◆ True

The biggest bird is the flightless ostrich, which can weigh more than eight times as much as the heaviest flying bird.

5 **Which of these is a male turkey's call?**

◆ Gobbling

The male wild turkey is a huge, highly ornamented bird that struts around while making gobbling calls.

4 **What bird likes to impale its prey on thorns to save and eat later?**

◆ Red-backed shrike

They behave like hawks, seizing lizards, mice, and large insects, then tearing them apart with their hooked bills.

6 How big is the wingspan of the wandering albatross?

● 11 ft (3.5 m)

It's the widest wingspan of any bird. Wandering albatrosses only breed every other year, because rearing a chick takes a year.

7 What bird is nicknamed the American eagle?

◆ Bald eagle

It builds the largest nest of any bird, weighing in at over 6,000 lb (2,700 kg)—that's more than a rhinoceros.

8 How can cassowaries cause severe injury?

● With their feet

They have three toes on each foot. The innermost toe has a sharp claw, which can inflict lethal wounds.

9 How many fish can an Atlantic puffin carry in its bill?

● Up to 30

Puffins have surprisingly spacious beaks and they usually hunt small fish like herring or sand eels. They can dive to depths of 200 feet for their food.

10 How many starlings might gather to roost for the night in the winter?

● 1.5 million

An estimated 150 million Eurasian starlings live in North America, all descended from just 60 birds released in New York in 1890.

Podium!

Bronze: 1–5 correct answers
Silver: 6–8 correct answers
Gold: 9–10 correct answers

Conservation

Conserve your energy and get your thinking cap on, this quiz will help you learn about our world!

1 What is conservation?
- ◆ Protecting things found in nature
- ▲ Burning fossil fuels
- ● Hunting animals

2 How much has the Bornean orangutans' habitat been reduced by over the last 20 years?
- ◆ 25 percent
- ▲ 40 percent
- ● 55 percent

3 What is affecting polar bears' ability to find food?
- ◆ Ice cover is diminishing
- ▲ There are fewer seals
- ● They are being hunted to extinction

4 What happens to birds affected by oil spillages?
- ◆ They look dirty
- ▲ They lose their appetites
- ● Their waterproof plumage is destroyed

5 **What is the IUCN Red List?**

◆ A list of threatened species

▲ A list of the hottest places on Earth

● A list of countries with endangered animals

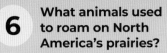

6 **What animals used to roam on North America's prairies?**

◆ Bears and bison

▲ Lions and tigers

● Elephants and giraffes

7 **By what date were passenger pigeons extinct in the wild?**

◆ 1800

▲ 1900

● 2000

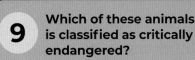

9 **Which of these animals is classified as critically endangered?**

◆ Black rhinoceros

▲ Blue whale

● Giant panda

■ Arctic wolf

Did you know?

In 1900, there were fewer than 20 Southern white rhinos and they lived on a reserve in South Africa. In 2020, there were 10,080 mature individuals in the wild.

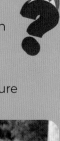

8 **True or false: Overfishing also affects animals not in the sea.**

◆ True

▲ False

10 **What can help a species from becoming extinct?**

◆ Captive breeding

▲ Leaving it alone

● Giving it cuddles

Turn to page 116 for the answers!

Conservation Answers

1 **What is conservation?**
◆ Protecting things found in nature

It requires the sensible use of all Earth's natural resources: water, soil, minerals, wildlife, and forests.

2 **How much has the Bornean orangutans' habitat been reduced by over the last 20 years?**
● 55 percent

Their populations are critically endangered as a result of hunting and deforestation.

3 **What is affecting polar bears' ability to find food?**
◆ Ice cover is diminishing

Polar bears use winter sea ice as a platform for catching seals.

4 **What happens to birds affected by oil spillages?**
● Their waterproof plumage is destroyed

Oil spills are toxic to wildlife. Without treatment, affected birds can die.

5 **What is the IUCN Red List?**
◆ A list of threatened species

The International Union for Conservation of Nature's extinction risk assessments are used to help make conservation decisions globally.

6 **What animals used to roam on North America's prairies?**

◆ Bears and bison

The prairies are now almost entirely devoted to cereal farming. The original grassland habitat has largely disappeared.

7 **By what date were passenger pigeons extinct in the wild?**

▲ 1900

The last individual bird, named Martha, died in captivity in 1941 at the Cincinnati Zoo.

8 **True or false: Overfishing also affects animals not in the sea.**

◆ True

Fish play a key part in many food chains, and when their numbers fall the effects are also felt by numerous fish-eating birds.

9 **Which of these animals is classified as critically endangered?**

◆ Black rhinoceros

The blue whale is classified as endangered, the giant panda is classified as vulnerable, and the Arctic wolf is classified as of least concern.

10 **What can help a species from becoming extinct?**

◆ Captive breeding

In 1982, captive breeding saved the California condor. At the time, there were only about 24 left in the wild. The total population is now over 430, with more than half this number flying free.

Podium!
Bronze: 1–5 correct answers
Silver: 6–8 correct answers
Gold: 9–10 correct answers

Predators

Sink your teeth into this tough quiz as you hunt for the correct answers.

1 Which of these animals is not a predator?
- ◆ Zebra
- ▲ Lion
- ● Hyena

2 True or false: A Nile crocodile will kill and eat almost anything.
- ◆ True
- ▲ False

3 What does an opossum do to escape predators?
- ◆ Runs away
- ▲ Plays dead
- ● Growls loudly

4 Which of these animals is not an apex predator?
- ◆ Saltwater crocodile
- ▲ Komodo dragon
- ● Giant squid

5 How do gerbils flee from predators?
- ◆ With running leaps
- ▲ By flying into the air
- ● By burrowing into the sand

Did you know?

The Etruscan shrew eats twice its weight every day in crickets, cockroaches, and spiders. Since their prey is nearly as big as they are, shrews have to attack fast.

6 Which of these was the largest prehistoric predator in the sea?
◆ Plesiosaur
▲ Mosasaurus
● Megalodon

7 How do pufferfish puff themselves up to scare off predators?
◆ They take in lots of air
▲ They eat as much as possible
● They gulp in lots of water

8 Put these animals in the correct order in the food chain, with the apex predator last.
◆ Grasshopper
▲ Hawk
● Frog
■ Snake

9 True or false: The African bullfrog will sometimes eat its own young.
◆ True
▲ False

Scan the QR code for a Kahoot! about predators.

10 What are a Komodo dragon's teeth like?
◆ Serrated steak knives
▲ Sharp points
● Smooth blades

Turn to page 120 for the answers!

Predators
Answers

1 Which of these animals is not a predator?

◆ Zebra

Lions and hyenas hunt zebras. Groups of spotted hyenas are capable of driving a lion off its kill and claiming it for their own.

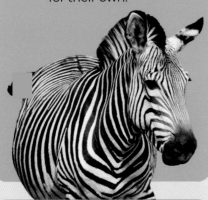

2 True or false: A Nile crocodile will kill and eat almost anything?

◆ True

It specializes in ambush tactics, lurking in pools and rivers. Bursting up from the water, it drags its victim under before tearing it apart.

3 What does an opossum do to escape predators?

▲ Plays dead

Most predators like to eat live food and will lose interest in animals that are already dead. This has become known as "playing possum."

4 Which of these animals is not an apex predator?

● Giant squid

Giant squid are predators because they eat fish and shellfish, but are not apex predators because they are themselves preyed on by sperm whales.

5 How do gerbils flee from predators?

◆ With running leaps

The Indian gerbil can leap about 15 ft (4.5 m).

6 Which of these was the largest prehistoric predator in the sea?

● Megalodon

This prehistoric shark from over 2.6 million years ago preyed on fish, seals, whales, and other sea creatures.

7 How do pufferfish puff themselves up to scare off predators?

● They gulp in lots of water

Once swollen they can barely move, but their spines make them practically impossible to attack.

8 Put these animals in the correct order in the food chain, with the apex predator last.

◆ Grasshopper
● Frog
■ Snake
▲ Hawk

Food chains always end with an apex predator, which is not eaten by anything else.

9 True or false: The African bullfrog will sometimes eat its own young.

◆ True

It's a predator who will eat almost any animal that can fit in its huge mouth, including its own young.

10 What are a Komodo dragon's teeth like?

◆ Serrated steak knives

They have up to 60 curved teeth, which can slice through the tough hide and flesh of prey.

Podium!

Bronze: 1–5 correct answers
Silver: 6–8 correct answers
Gold: 9–10 correct answers

Record Breakers

Can you break a world record for answering these quiz questions? Get ready . . . Go!

1 What's the tallest animal in the world?
- ◆ Gorilla
- ▲ Elephant
- ● Hippo
- ■ Giraffe

2 True or false: Cheetahs can reach speeds of over 62 mph (100 kph).
- ◆ True
- ▲ False

3 What's the name of the smallest bird in the world?
- ◆ Lesser spotted waspbird
- ▲ Bee hummingbird
- ● Flycatcher
- ■ Microscopic eagle

4 How heavy was the largest giant clam ever found?
- ◆ 220 lb (100 kg)
- ▲ 440 lb (200 kg)
- ● 660 lb (300 kg)
- ■ 1,100 lb (500 kg)

5 True or false: The smallest shark in the world is the deep-sea elfshark.

◆ True

▲ False

6 What type of animal is the orca the largest of?

◆ Whale

▲ Shark

● Dolphin

■ Swordfish

7 Why is Madame Berthe's mouse lemur a record breaker?

◆ It's the loudest mouse lemur

▲ It's the smallest primate

● It's the fastest primate

■ It's the most venomous mammal

8 What's the name of the largest-known crustacean?

◆ Japanese spider crab

▲ German ant lobster

● Venezuelan moth shrimp

■ Somalian louse barnacle

9 Which animal is probably the largest that ever lived?

◆ African elephant

▲ Tyrannosaurus rex

● Blue whale

10 What is the oldest-known land animal alive today?

◆ Elephant

▲ Hippo

● Tortoise

Turn to page 124 for the answers!

Record Breakers

Answers

1 **What's the tallest animal in the world?**

■ Giraffe

Measuring up to 19.7 ft (6 m) tall, giraffes also have incredibly long tongues of up to 17.7 in (45 cm).

2 **True or false: Cheetahs can reach speeds of over 62 mph (100 kph).**

◆ True

Cheetahs are famous as the world's fastest land animals. They can reach this speed for 10 to 20 seconds.

4 **How heavy was the largest giant clam ever found?**

● 660 lb (300 kg)

These giant clams are heavier than two fully grown giant pandas.

3 **What's the name of the smallest bird in the world?**

▲ Bee hummingbird

The bee hummingbird is only 2–2.4 in (5–6 cm) long—that's only slightly bigger than the size of an ostrich's eye!

5 True or false: The smallest shark in the world is the deep-sea elfshark.

▲ False

The smallest shark is the deep-sea dwarf lanternshark. It is just 6.7 in (17 cm) long.

6 What type of animal is the orca the largest of?

● Dolphin

Measuring up to 32 ft (9.8 m) long, this powerful predator is actually a giant dolphin.

7 Why is Madame Berthe's mouse lemur a record breaker?

▲ It's the smallest primate

This tiny primate's body only measures up to 3.7 in (9.5 cm) long, but its tail can be an additional 5.5 in (14 cm).

8 What's the name of the largest-known crustacean?

◆ Japanese spider crab

This huge crab's spindly legs can measure up to 5 ft (1.5 m) long!

9 Which animal is probably the largest that ever lived?

● Blue whale

Adults are up to 107 ft (32.6 m) long, but their calves are also huge at 23 ft (7 m) long.

10 What is the oldest-known land animal alive today?

● Tortoise

Jonathan the tortoise was born in 1832, making him 190 years old in 2022.

Podium!
Bronze: 1–5 correct answers
Silver: 6–8 correct answers
Gold: 9–10 correct answers

Glossary

Captivity
Animals in captivity are held by humans so that they cannot escape, such as in zoos.

Cartilage
Strong and flexible connective tissue found throughout the body, and covering joints.

Dormancy
A time where growth, development, and physical activity are temporarily suspended to save energy.

Echolocation
The process of using sound waves to detect the location of objects.

Insectivorous
Animals that only eat insects.

Marsupials
Mammals that raise their newborn offspring inside an external pouch at the front or underside of their body, such as a kangaroo.

Omnivore
A human or animal that eats both plants and animals.

Retractable
If something is retractable, it can be drawn back in, like a set of cat's claws.

Termite
Small and soft-bodied insects living in large colonies. They can be highly destructive to trees and timber.

Venomous
Venomous animals are ones that secrete venom and inject it into the body of another animal or human. For example, using fangs or stingers.

Vertebrate
Any animal that has a spine. It is the opposite of an invertebrate.

Picture Credits

The publisher would like to thank the following for their kind permission to reproduce their photographs:

(Key: a-above; b-below/bottom; c-centre; f-far; l-left; r-right; t-top)

2 Dreamstime.com: Mgkuijpers (clb); Pixworld (cr). 3 Dreamstime.com: Stu Porter / Stuporter (cb). 4 Dreamstime.com: Jerryway (cr). 10 123RF.com: Tim Hester / timhester (cl). Getty Images / iStock: OscarEspinosa (cr). 11 Getty Images / iStock: Mark Kostich (clb). 12 Dorling Kindersley: Jerry Young (br). 13 Getty Images / iStock: Mark Kostich (cla). 14 Dreamstime.com: Isselee (br); Wei-chuan Liu / Rebelml (bc). 15 Dreamstime.com: Tomonishi (cla). 16 Dreamstime.com: Nilanjan Bhattacharya (bl). 19 Getty Images: Frans Lemmens (cra). 20 Dreamstime.com: Annaav (crb). 21 Dorling Kindersley: Alan Murphy (tl). Dreamstime.com: Anek Suwannaphoom (cra). 22 123RF.com: smileus (crb). 23 123RF.com: Michael Zysman / deserttrends (clb). Dreamstime.com: Isselee (cra). 25 Dreamstime.com: Srisakorn Wonglakorn (cl). 26 Dreamstime.com: Daniel Prudek (cr). 27 123RF.com: Eric Isselee / isselee (tr). 28 123RF.com: Tom Tietz / natureguy (cl). Dreamstime.com: Abeselom Zerit (bl). 29 Dorling Kindersley: Blackpool Zoo (cra). 30 Dreamstime.com: Pedro Pereira (bl). Getty Images / iStock: mccluremr (cr). 31 Dreamstime.com: Wrangel (bl). 32 Dreamstime.com: Isselee (cr). 33 Dreamstime.com: Timbalcomb (bl). 34 Dreamstime.com: Cathy Keifer (cl). 35 Dreamstime.com: Orlandin (cr). 36 Dreamstime.com: Ziga Camernik (cra). 38 Dreamstime.com: Gary Parker (bl); Shawn Jackson / Shawnjackson (crb). 39 Getty Images: Sjoerd Bosch (cl). 40 Dreamstime.com: Seadam (cr). 41 Dreamstime.com: Robert Randall (cr). 42 Dreamstime.com: Dream69 (bl). 43 Dreamstime.com: Obrien63 (crb); Michael Valos (bl). 44 Dreamstime.com: Jamen Percy / Jamenpercy (cr). Getty Images / iStock: vladoskan (cl). 45 Dreamstime.com: Karl Daniels / Webphoto99 (cra). 46 Dreamstime.com: Isselee (bl); Razihusin (cl); Mgkuijpers (crb). 47 Dreamstime.com: Eric Isselee (ca). 48 Dreamstime.com: Jesse Kraft (cr). 49 Dorling Kindersley: Jerry Young (cr). Dreamstime.com: Coffeemill (cla). 50 Dreamstime.com: Jerryway (clb). 51 Dreamstime.com: Amwu (bl); Vladimir Melnikov (crb). 52 Dreamstime.com: Isselee (cr). 53 Dreamstime.com: Mirror Images (bl). 54 Dreamstime.com: Kirsten Karius (cr). 55 Dreamstime.com: Isselee (cra). 56 Dreamstime.com: Anna Artamonova (cr); Jnjhuz (cla). 57 Getty Images / iStock: AlasdairJames (tr). 58 Dreamstime.com: Rusty Dodson (br). 59 Alamy Stock Photo: Big Pants Productions (bl). Dreamstime.com: Victortyakht (crb). 61 Getty Images / iStock: ookawaphoto (cr). 62 Dreamstime.com: Kotomiti_okuma (br). 63 Dreamstime.com: Mikelane45 (cl); Alexey Sedov (tr). 65 123RF.com: Richard Lindie (cra). Dreamstime.com: Andreanita (tr). 66 Dreamstime.com: Karin Van Ijzendoorn (cr). 67 123RF.com: Eric Isselee / isselee (cl). Dreamstime.com: Leonmaraisphoto (tl). 68 Dreamstime.com: Pixworld (br). 69 Dreamstime.com: Neal Cooper (bl). 70 Dorling Kindersley: Jerry Young (clb). 73 Dreamstime.com: Karin59 (bl). 74 123RF.com: wrangel (crb). 76 Dreamstime.com: Steve Allen (crb). 77 Fotolia: MATTHIJS KUIJPERS / mgkuijpers (cr). 78 Dorling Kindersley: Natural History Museum, London (br). Dreamstime.com: Isselee (crb). Getty Images / iStock: lindsay_imagery (cl). 79 Dreamstime.com: Dan Rieck (cra). 80 Dreamstime.com: Isselee (c, crb). 81 Dreamstime.com: Arsty (cla). 82 Alamy Stock Photo: D. Hurst (cr). Dreamstime.com: Irina Kozhemyakina / Ir717 (br). 83 Dreamstime.com: Szymon Bartosz (cl). 84 Dreamstime.com: Slowmotiongli (cr). 85 Dreamstime.com: Jeff097 (clb); Glenn Nagel (cra). 86 Getty Images: Westend61 (crb). 87 Dreamstime.com: Lunamarina (cla); Photomyeye (cr). 88 Dreamstime.com: Kiankhoon (cr). 89 Dreamstime.com: Photomyeye (cl). 90 Dorling Kindersley: Jerry Young (cl). Fotolia: Eric Isselee (bl). 92 Dreamstime.com: Ashleylswanson (crb). 94 Dreamstime.com: Isselee (cr). 95 123RF.com: tudor antonel adrian / tony4urban (cr). 96 Dreamstime.com: Isselee (cr); Mikelane45 (cl). 97 Dreamstime.com: Alex Lopatko (cr); Maryna Rayimova (bl); Chris Moncrieff (cla). 98 Dreamstime.com: Eric Issele / Isselee (bl). 99 123RF.com: Eric Isselee / isselee (br). Dreamstime.com: Chase Dekker (crb); Frank Fichtmueller (cla). 100 Dorling Kindersley: Cotswold Wildlife Park (cl). 101 Dreamstime.com: Dmitry Maslov (clb). 102 Dreamstime.com: Seadam (bl). 103 Dreamstime.com: Andrey Armyagov / Cookelma (cl). 106 Dreamstime.com: Mark Turner (b). 107 Dreamstime.com: Khunaspix (cra); Jeff Whyte (bl). 109 Dreamstime.com: Isselee (tc); Pipa100 (cl). 110 Dreamstime.com: Pixworld (bl). Getty Images / iStock: mauribo (cr). 111 123RF.com: Andrea Izzotti (cr). Fotolia: Stefan Zeitz / Lux (c). 112 Dorling Kindersley: E. J. Peiker (br). Getty Images / iStock: mauribo (cr). 114 Dreamstime.com: Sergey Uryadnikov / Surz01 (bl); Steven Davis / Theseedco (cr). 115 Dreamstime.com: Hedrus (cra). 116 Dreamstime.com: Petemasty (br). 117 Dorling Kindersley: Gary Hanna / Mattscott / Dreamstime.com (bl). Dreamstime.com: Svetlana Foote (cr). 118 Dreamstime.com: Marion Wear (clb). 118-119 Dreamstime.com: Isselee (bc). 120 Dorling Kindersley: Jerry Young (clb). Dreamstime.com: Marcin Ciesielski / Sylwia Cisek (br). 121 Dreamstime.com: Tariq Hameed Sulemani (tl). 122 Dreamstime.com: Stu Porter / Stuporter (cr); Tinamou (br). 123 Dreamstime.com: Artushfoto (clb); Slowmotiongli (cra). 124 Dorling Kindersley: Jerry Young (br). Getty Images / iStock: linephoto (clb). 125 Dreamstime.com: Andrey Armyagov / Cookelma (tr); Kotomiti_okuma (br). 128 Alamy Stock Photo: D. Hurst (crb). Dreamstime.com: Nilanjan Bhattacharya (cra). Fotolia: Stefan Zeitz / Lux (cl)

Cover images: Front: Dreamstime.com: Ammit tr, Isselee crb; Back: Dorling Kindersley: Natural History Museum, London tl; Dreamstime.com: Annaav tr

All other images © Dorling Kindersley

Dorling Kindersley would like to thank Morten Versvik, Ritesh Maisuria, Perla P. Pinto, Francisco Bembibre, and Craig Narveson at Kahoot! DK also thanks David McDonald, James McKeag, and Isabelle Merry for design assistance, Elizabeth Cook for editorial help, and Cathriona Hickey for fact checking.

DK | Penguin Random House

Senior Art Editor Anna Formanek
Cover design James McKeag and Isabelle Merry
US Editors Susan Hobbs and Lori Hand
Senior Production Editor Jennifer Murray
Senior Production Controller Lloyd Robertson
Managing Editor Paula Regan
Managing Art Editor Jo Connor
Publishing Director Mark Searle

Packaged for DK by Dynamo Limited

First American Edition, 2023
Published in the United States by DK Publishing
1745 Broadway, 20th Floor,
New York, NY 10019

Page design copyright © 2023 Dorling Kindersley Limited
DK, a Division of Penguin Random House LLC
23 24 25 26 27 10 9 8 7 6 5 4 3 2 1
001–334339–Sept/2023

A CIP catalog record for this book
is available from the Library of Congress.
ISBN: 978-0-7440-7664-6

Printed and bound in China

For the curious
www.dk.com
www.kahoot.com

create.kahoot.it/profiles/dk-learning-us

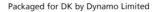

MIX
Paper | Supporting
responsible forestry
FSC™ C018179

This book was made with Forest
Stewardship Council™ certified
paper—one small step in DK's
commitment to a sustainable future.
For more information go to
www.dk.com/our-green-pledge